INVESTMENT AND ECONOMIC REFORM IN LATIN AMERICA

Graciela Moguillansky and Ricardo Bielschowsky (with Claudio Pini)

UNITED NATIONS

**ECONOMIC COMMISSION FOR
LATIN AMERICA AND THE CARIBBEAN**

Santiago, Chile, 2001

Libros de la CEPAL

63

This book has been prepared by Graciela Moguillansky, Economic Affair Officer at ECLAC Santiago and Ricardo Bielschowsky, Economic Affair Officer at ECLAC Brasilia, and published by the Economic Commission for Latin America and the Caribbean (ECLAC).

This book has been published as part of a project funded by the Netherlands Ministry for Development Cooperation and with contributions from the International Development Research Centre of Canada (IDRC) and the Swedish International Development Agency.

Cover illustration and design by Andrés Hannach.
Composition by Gilabert&Domeyko Ltda.

United Nations Publication
LC/G.2128-P
ISBN: 92-1-121294-4
Copyright © United Nations, May 2001. All rights reserved
Sales No. E.01.II.G.21
Printed in Chile

TABLE OF CONTENTS

FOREWORD

At the start of the new decade, the debate on economic policy centres on the consequence of the reforms implemented in Latin America and the Caribbean in the last two decades. Trade and financial liberalization and the privatization of production activities have radically altered the rules of the game governing labour and business. The macroeconomic policy changes that accompanied or preceded the reforms sometimes strengthened the latter's specific objectives, especially the growth of exports, but on other occasions they had the opposite effect. That combination of factors prompted the emergence of new market structures and transformations in microeconomic behaviour.

Assessing the effects of the reforms on economic growth, employment and income distribution is of more than academic interest. Governments, political parties and social actors require a thorough evaluation of the results, so as to devise or propose policies that complement the reforms or counter their unwanted consequences. The Economic Commission for Latin America and the Caribbean (ECLAC) actively participates in this process.

This book is part of a project carried out by ECLAC, in conjunction with researchers from nine countries, to study the impact of the reforms. Directed by Dr. Barbara Stallings, the project has produced 14 books and 70 working papers. The summary appears in the first volume, entitled *Growth, Employment and Equity: The Impact of the Economic Reforms in Latin America and the Caribbean*. It is complemented by four issue-specific volumes analysing investment, technological change, employment and equity. Additionally, another nine country volumes examine the particular characteristics of the reforms in Argentina, Bolivia, Brazil, Chile, Colombia, Costa Rica, Jamaica, Mexico and Peru. The working papers are available at ECLAC's web site (www.cepal.cl).

One feature of the project that distinguishes it from other comparative studies of economic reform is that it specifically addresses the interaction between macroeconomic and microeconomic processes. To understand the impact of the reforms more fully, it is necessary to disaggregate the regional level and to study the differences between countries and in the microeconomic behaviour of firms according to sector, size and ownership. The globalization of the economy and government policies such as structural reform affect different countries and groups of firms in different ways. Some have been able to exploit the new opportunities, while the situation of others has deteriorated. The outcome of such developments gives rise to aggregate trends that others have observed and measured, but to design economic policy measures and improve future performance, it is essential to know what underlies those aggregates.

In this book, ECLAC economists Graciela Moguillansky and Ricardo Bielschowsky analyze the investment process, using the methodology just mentioned. Unlike traditional analyses of the determinants of investment, which have tended to rely largely on macroeconomic variables, Moguillansky and Bielschowsky's study attempts to link macroeconomic aspects to sectoral, microeconomic and institutional factors. Thus, they examine the impact of structural reform, institutional change, market structures and the role of agents (both domestic and foreign private agents and the State) in conjunction with the increasingly important legal and regulatory aspects. This approach represents a major step forward in the development of a new methodology for analysing the complex determinants of investment.

A second noteworthy feature of the book is its contribution to the understanding of the investment process in the context of the transition set in train by economic reform, by identifying the phases of the investment cycle and the way firms adapt to institutional change. The study looks at both permanent and transitory factors, the latter stemming from the effects of reform policies, which have a different impact at each phase of the investment cycle. An analysis of sectoral investment trends serves to discern patterns in the allocation of capital resources after reform and the strengths and vulnerabilities thus generated, which help to explain the existence of obstacles to the attainment of a high sustained growth rate in the region.

As well as making a methodological and substantive contribution, the book adds new material to the existing stock of empirical information by supplying quantitative data on the distribution of investment by sector for each of the countries examined and a comparison of changes in legislation and sectoral regulations in different countries of the region. This material was not previously available and will without doubt be useful for those who profess an interest in this subject area.

ECLAC could not have carried out a project of this scale without the cooperation of many individuals and institutions. We wish to thank the researchers that participated in each of the nine countries, as well as the coordinators of the thematic and national volumes. We are also indebted to the members of the project's External Advisory Committee: Nancy Birdsall, Director of Economic Programs at the Carnegie Endowment for International Peace; René Cortázar, Executive Director of Chilean National Television; Norman Hicks, senior economist at the World Bank; Juan Antonio Morales, President of the Central Bank of Bolivia; Pitou van Dijck, Professor of Economics at the University of Amsterdam; and Dorothea Werneck, Executive Director of the Brazilian Agency for Export Promotion.

External financing came from a number of international donors. First, we wish to recognize the central role of the Netherlands Ministry for Development Cooperation, which provided the project's basic donation. The International Development Research Centre of Canada (IDRC) also made a substantial contribution that allowed us to expand the scope of the project significantly. These two sources were supplemented with funds from the Ford Foundation and the Swedish International Development Agency. We offer our deepest thanks to all the donors, without whose support this project would not have been possible.

JOSÉ ANTONIO OCAMPO
EXECUTIVE SECRETARY
ECONOMIC COMMISSION FOR LATIN AMERICA AND THE CARIBBEAN

PREFACE

This book presents the findings of research into the effects of economic reform on investment. The research forms part of a larger multinational project, "Growth, employment and equity: the impact of economic reforms in Latin America and the Caribbean", carried out by the United Nations Economic Commission for Latin America and the Caribbean (ECLAC) and researchers from nine countries in the region.

In line with the other parts of the project, the research focused on analysing the interaction of macroeconomic, sectoral and microeconomic variables affected by the reforms. As a result, we have gained a better understanding of what influences private and public actors' decisions with regard to resource allocation. The study is limited to those countries which have microeconomic and sectoral information on investment or in which it was possible to compile such information. Hence we looked at eight of the nine countries in the larger project: Argentina, Bolivia, Brazil, Chile, Colombia, Costa Rica, Mexico and Peru.

With the exception of Colombia and Costa Rica, the statistical and national accounting institutions in the countries do not disaggregate investment accounts by destination. The consultants involved in the project therefore had to use microeconomic and sectoral information provided by firms and government sectoral organizations.

Given the complexity of the subject, we chose a number of sectors which played an important role in the productive apparatus and in infrastructure services throughout the period studied, the 1990s. In the productive category, we chose mining, industry and hydrocarbon production. In the case of the first two, we were able to use information on investment published in company annual reports and provided by official sectoral bodies, including ministries and related units. The analysis of the industrial sector was based on annual surveys from national statistical offices and on organizations, such as the Central Bank of Mexico which carries out surveys on the capital stock in that country.

13

We chose three infrastructure sectors for analysis: electricity, telecommunications and highways. The first two were affected by the sectoral reforms and privatizations which took place throughout the 1990s, while private-sector participation in the third began to increase towards the end of the decade. In all three cases statistics on investment were taken from annual company reports and from official institutions, such as ministries of energy, public works, transport and communications.

This study would not have been possible without the collaboration of many people. The contributions of Barbara Stallings (coordinator of the global project), Jorge Katz (coordinator of the module on technological change), Jurgen Weller (employment coordinator), Samuel Morley (equity coordinator) and our colleague Wilson Peres were invaluable in developing the methodology and helping us to achieve a multidimensional focus. In addition, ideas for combining micro- and macroeconomic analysis, which are the result of previous research by Jorge Katz, were extremely useful in designing the research methodology.

Coodination and supervision of the sectoral studies in the countries were the responsibility of the following people: Bernardo Kosacoff, of the ECLAC office in Buenos Aires, Argentina; Gover Barja, associate professor in the M.A. program on development at the Catholic University, Bolivia; Juan Mauricio Ramírez, economist at Fedesarrollo, Colombia; Jorge Mattar, of the subregional office of ECLAC in Mexico; and Humberto Campodónico, economist at the Centre for Studies and Promotion of Development (DESCO) in Peru. The authors of this book coordinated the sectoral studies in Chile and Brazil.

The studies which provided the foundation for the sectoral chapters were the responsibility of: Luis Abugattás, Gover Barja, Ricardo Bielschowsky, Roberto Bisang, José Antonio Cordero, Georgina Gómez, Gerardo Mendiola, Juan Carlos Moreno-Brid, Juan Mauricio Ramírez and Liliana Núñez, for the industrial sector; Víctor Ayala, Humberto Campodónico, Virginia de Moori, José Clemente de Oliveira, Israel Fainboim, Nicolás Gadano, Graciela Moguillansky, Carlos Jorge Rodriguez, Sebastião Soares and Ramón Torres, for the mining and hydrocarbon sectors; Gover Barja, Ricardo Bielschowsky, Humberto Campodónico, Marcelo Celani, José Antonio Cordero, Ricardo Delgado, Rebeca Escobar, Israel Fainboim, Graciela Moguillansky, Carlos Jorge Rodríguez, Víctor Rodríguez, Carlos Romero and Isaac Scheinver, for the infrastructure sectors.

The authors would like to thank those who gave invaluable comments on preliminary versions of the book: Hector Assael, Renato Baumann, Alvaro Díaz, João Ferraz, Ricardo Ffrench-Davis, Stephany Griffith-Jones, André Hofman, Oscar Muñoz, Carlos Mussi, Jaime Ros, Osvaldo Rosales, Rogerio Studart, Anabelle Ulate and Pitou Van Dyck. Finally, we greatly appreciate the secretarial assistance of Ximena Sánchez and María Eugenia Johnson, the translation of Holly Mikkelson and Mary Stainer, and the English editing of Jennifer Hoover. The authors alone are responsible for the final product.

INTRODUCTION

The recent economic reforms in Latin America undoubtedly represent a milestone in the region's history and account for many of the transformations that occurred there in the 1990s. In this context, it is important to ask what has happened with investment. Is investment exceeding historical levels? Has it been allocated to the right sectors to boost competitiveness and ensure steady growth? Or have the reforms served to weaken the investment process, in the context of the globalization and economic internationalization that characterize today's world? These are the principal questions this study attempts to answer.

On reviewing the Latin American literature on the subject, it is possible to find studies that examine the effects of instability and adjustment on capital formation in their treatment of the main problems of the 1980s.[1] In contrast, studies on economic reforms carried out in the 1990s look at their repercussions on growth, but they do not pay much attention to investment, on the assumption that its dynamic nature can be taken for granted.[2] Unlike the latter group of studies, this one examines various aspects of macroeconomic policy and economic reform, while at the same time considering the process of capital formation from the macroeconomic, sectoral and microeconomic standpoints. In view of the fact that one of the principal obstacles to development and sustained growth in the region throughout its history has been external restrictions and a limited capacity to generate foreign exchange, it is particularly important to determine where capital is being channelled within the framework of the market-opening strategy. This book considers eight countries, large and small: Argentina, Bolivia, Brazil, Chile, Colombia,

---

1 See, for example, ECLAC (1992), Cardoso (1993), Corbo and Rojas (1993), Bacha (1993), Servén and Solimano (1993), ECLAC (1996), Schmidt Hebbel, Servén and Solimano (1996).

2 See, for example, Edwards (1995), Lora and Barrera (1998), Fernandez-Arias and Montiel (1998).

Costa Rica, Mexico and Peru. In the 1990s these countries, which together account for 80% of the population and nearly 90% of the regional gross domestic product (GDP), consolidated their reforms or initiated the process.

The analysis is based, in part, on 40 working papers related to various sectors, including a variety of industrial branches –at the three-digit level of the International Standard Industrial Classification of all economic activities (ISIC)– as well as mining, hydrocarbons and the infrastructure sectors most directly associated with competitiveness (electricity, telecommunications and highways). This material has been published by ECLAC; the respective bibliographic references appear in each chapter.

Only in a few cases do the statistics come from public institutions (e.g., the countries' statistics bureaux, ministries or central banks); most have been generated by consultants who developed the series and carried out the specific studies of each sector. The research was conducted with a relatively uniform methodology, thereby ensuring reasonable homogeneity in the different studies.

The analysis focuses on three dimensions in particular: the macroeconomic dimension, which is normally considered in economic theory; the sectoral or mesoeconomic dimension, which brings institutional factors into play; and the microeconomic dimension, which centres on firms' investment strategies as they deal with change. The need to analyse these three dimensions stems from the fact that there is no consolidated approach with generalized behaviours that can be subsumed under a new single model of investment. On the contrary, we find changes at the macroeconomic level (with respect to policies and reforms) that elicit different reactions among firms throughout a transition period. This leads us to look at the microeconomic dimension, that is, the reactions of different types of firms, to distinguish their responses. In addition, these responses reflect institutional changes at the sectoral level, which also affect investment decisions. These changes translate into new rules of the game, causing firms to gradually adapt to signals that have turned out to be neither linear nor unidirectional. Finally, in the first stages of the process, the effects of the reforms, the macroeconomic policies and the new international context are not independent of each other, but rather interact in such a way that affects investment. We discuss these characteristics in more detail below.

We speak of a transition process for several reasons. In the first place, the countries that began their reforms in the 1990s (Argentina, Brazil, Colombia and Peru) have not had enough time to consolidate a new economic model, so investment decisions were made in the context of great uncertainty. Second, the reforms did not begin simultaneously on all fronts. In general, trade liberalization was the first measure, while labour reform and the privatization of public utilities were among the last to be adopted. Third, whereas in some countries all reforms were undertaken simultaneously (Argentina and Peru, beginning in 1990), in others the process developed slowly and in a different sequence, which prevented the reforms from maturing fully (Bolivia, Brazil and Costa Rica are good examples in this regard). Fourth, the reforms did not proceed in linear fashion, which meant that economic actors were exposed to changing rules of the game. Consider, for example, the tariff surcharges and other obstacles to international trade that cropped up anew in these countries after each balance-of-payments crisis.

Finally, the consolidation of the new market-oriented model –defined as the point at which new institutions have taken shape[3] – has been hindered by crises resulting from the internal and external imbalances that have continued to plague these countries in the period following the reforms. The existence of an open capital account and local financial systems with weak institutions not only contributed to this destabilization, but also cast doubt on macroeconomic policies and exposed the weakness of the reforms. The initial deregulation of various markets (financial, securities, public utilities and others) gave rise to a number of problems, and over time, governments were forced to regulate, modify and strengthen the relevant laws and institutions. The reforms were thus reoriented, which led to new uncertainty among firms. As a result, the behaviour of these actors has not yet been fully defined.

Firms have adapted to the changes in a variety of ways. In most countries, the economy has evolved from a closed system of protection, with strong State intervention, to a system characterized by openness, deregulation and privatization. Firms adapted to these changes to the extent they could, depending on their strength and their other microeconomic characteristics. It was much more difficult for small and medium-sized enterprises to respond to competition from imported goods in terms of quality and prices than it was for large enterprises or subsidiaries of transnational corporations.

Reactions also differed among economic sectors. In some countries, opening up the economy strengthened sectors that were involved in processing natural resources, while in others it favoured the clothing, automotive and electronics sectors. Companies with a long history in these industries took advantage of their knowledge of production processes and the market, which enabled them to grow and increase profitability. The same policies depressed many other sectors, such as machine tools, electric machinery manufacturing and the textile and clothing industries (see Katz, 1996; Kosacoff, 1998).

The nature of the period under study gave rise to a particular methodological approach that was basic to the research. Since the process in question has not yet solidified, we adopted an inductive method. In other words, we did not start with a theoretical model to try to see whether reality would conform to it; on the contrary, we analysed the behaviour of firms and sectors in different countries and tried to extrapolate certain general behaviours and responses with respect to investment. The behaviours may be consistent with those described in economic theory, or they may be more complex.

---

3   The consolidation stage of the economic liberalization model, linked to that of a new institutionality and a new role for the State, was defined earlier by Edwards (1995).

In studying the interactions among the macroeconomic, sectoral and microeconomic spheres, we analysed the links among policies, reforms and firms' reactions in each dimension.[4] Thus, in the macroeconomic analysis, not only did we consider the variables that all economic theories view as causal factors in investment (i.e., relative prices, demand behaviour and financing), but we also looked at the institutional changes that have affected the economy as a whole. No one denies that opening up trade created a new institutional framework, and that this reoriented investment decisions across sectors producing tradable and non-tradable goods, as well as among tradables. Moreover, financial liberalization provided a framework that made some investment projects feasible and others not, depending on the type of firm and the sector.

Other policies created a new institutional framework within specific sectors. In this connection, we analyse the effects of eliminating a broad range of sectoral policies originally aimed at the development of industrial activities; changes in mining legislation and in contracts for exploiting hydrocarbon reserves; and the impact of privatization and the new regulatory systems in place in infrastructure sectors. Finally, as is clear below, regional integration agreements established a new technological, financial and trade framework for some sectors of production, which had a decisive impact on business strategies and investment.

At the microeconomic level, studying how change is handled by different types of firms (namely, transnational corporations, large firms associated with economic groups and small and medium-sized enterprises) reveals that they do not all receive the same stimuli. This is because they are involved in different markets, or operate in segmented markets, and thus do not have equal access to them all. An example is firms' reactions to financial reforms and to the opening and development of the capital market. Whereas the large enterprises have had access to new, sophisticated financing instruments, small and medium-sized firms have not been able to take advantage of them, thus limiting their ability to develop investment projects. These different reactions to the same stimulus are also observed among firms in different sectors. For instance, trade liberalization affected exporters differently than it did sectors oriented towards the domestic market.

As the following diagram shows, the response to investment is more complex than could be represented by a single equation. The diagram outlines the three dimensions of analysis (the macroeconomic, sectoral and microeconomic dimensions) and the principal units of analysis (policies and reforms, sectors of economic activity and firms).

---

4   A noteworthy contribution on this point was the exchange of opinions with Jorge Katz, who is developing this framework of analysis (beginning with microeconomics) in his attempt to determine the impact of economic reforms on countries' technological behaviour (Katz, 1996 and 2000).

THE DETERMINANTS OF INVESTMENT

Macroeconomic level	Institutional incentives	Microeconomic level
POLICIES AND REFORMS	SECTORS	FIRMS

```
┌─────────────────────┐      ┌──────────────────────────┐      ┌──────────────────────┐
│ International factors│ ───→ │ Institutional changes    │      │ Historical evolution │
│                      │      │ Privatization            │      │ Microeconomic        │
│                      │      │ Regulation/deregulation  │      │ strength             │
│                      │      │ of markets               │      │                      │
└─────────────────────┘      └──────────────────────────┘      └──────────────────────┘
┌─────────────────────┐                                        │ Entry and exit of    │
│ Macroeconomic policy │                                        │ actors               │
│                      │      ┌──────────────────────────┐      │                      │
└─────────────────────┘      │ Institutional incentives │      │ Firm strategies      │
┌─────────────────────┐      │ Market failures          │      │ Technological        │
│ Economic reforms     │ ───→ │                          │      │ strategies           │
│                      │      └──────────────────────────┘      └──────────────────────┘
└─────────────────────┘      ┌──────────────────────────┐
┌─────────────────────┐      │ Market structure         │
│ Costs and relative  │ ←──  │ Degree of competition    │
│ prices              │      │                          │
│ Internal and external│     └──────────────────────────┘
│ demand              │      ┌──────────────────────────┐
│ Financing           │      │ Profitability            │
└─────────────────────┘      │ Risk                     │
┌─────────────────────┐      │ Strategic positioning    │
│ Degree of uncertainty│ ──  │                          │
└─────────────────────┘      └──────────────────────────┘
                                   ┌──────────────┐
                                   │ INVESTMENT   │
                                   └──────────────┘
```

In fact, it is as if we were dealing with a system of simultaneous equations with an interaction among the various types of firms, the business strategies of the various groups that make up the system and the institutional context in which they are operating, as well as macroeconomic policy, the new rules of the game embodied in the reforms and the changing characteristics of the international environment. These elements play a greater or lesser role depending on which sector is being analysed. In the model, expectations are constantly changing and are dependent on the evolution of the process, which is neither linear nor unidirectional.

In the system described above, we would have to consider the following circumstances:

i)   Demand, relative prices, costs and financing are not exogenous variables, but are affected by factors related to institutional changes, macroeconomic policy and changes in the international context (see the boxes in the above diagram corresponding to the macroeconomic level). The investment functions of some firms could be subject to financing restrictions, while those of others may not be.[5] Moreover, no single interest rate prevails in

---

5   An analysis of the specificity of the problem in developing countries can be found in Nissanke (1996).

the investment process, as it is possible to distinguish between firms with access to a domestic interest rate and others with access to the international rate, not to mention other distinctions.

ii) Firms' certainty is affected by macroeconomic conditions, by reforms and by changes in the international context. The entire reform process was a time of uncertainty, from the moment the reforms were launched until they began to take root. The degree of instability and volatility of prices, how much confidence people had in the new rules and the impact of international financial crises on the confidence of foreign investors all determine the timing of the decision to invest.[6]

iii) Behaviour within each sector is affected by macroeconomic factors and by the specific reforms taking place in the sector, such as privatizations and the regulation or deregulation of markets (see the boxes corresponding to the sectoral level in the diagram).

iv) These sectoral changes alter the existing degree of market competition, which affects the structure and organization of an industry. In some sectors, the competition is the direct result of liberalizing trade, since allowing external trade transformed traditionally oligopolistic markets into competitive ones. In other sectors, it was the privatization process that allowed new firms in. The manner in which privatization takes place, in turn, determines how competitive a market is. In some markets, special investment incentives were created, while in others, serious market failures have impeded proper functioning, as not all countries established appropriate conditions for competition during sector-level reforms. These situations were not static, however; they were affected by the introduction of regulatory instruments and mechanisms and by the business strategies pursued by new actors. The amount of competition in a given sector was a function of the contrast between the market power of business and the power of the regulatory body.

v) Because of the heterogeneity among the firms facing these changes, there is no single firm or representative sector function; various functions exist at the same time to strike a balance between the benefits expected of the projects and the costs and risks they imply. A given firm's response depends directly on its microeconomic strength and its history; some win and others lose in the process.[7] Business strategies both respond to and affect the degree of competition that exists in markets (see the boxes corresponding to the microeconomic level in the diagram).

vi) Finally, the equation between profit, risk and the requirements of a firm's strategic positioning determines the moment when an investment is actually made.

---

6   See the theoretical studies of Dixit (1989), Pindyck (1988, 1990, and 1993) and Caballero and Pindyck (1996).

7   These elements are derived from developments in the evolutionist school (see Nelson, 1991) and the interpretations Katz (1996 and 2000) and Kosacoff (1998) have made of microeconomics in Latin America.

Given the complexity of the analytical model and the inability to predict the direction and magnitude of the effects involved, we move from the microeconomic to the sectoral and then to the macroeconomic levels, but we also study the reverse direction of causality. The results of this analysis are described in the chapters on the investment behaviour of the different sectors.

This book has five chapters. The first chapter discusses firms' adaptation to change, examining statistics at the aggregate and sectoral levels. The first section of the chapter presents the conceptualization of the "investment phases" of the period following the reforms, analysing the impact of the macroeconomic context on each phase. The second section looks at trends in sectoral investment, introducing the analysis of several "transitory factors" as crucial determinants of the investment process.

The second chapter covers capital formation in the industrial sector. Industry was hit hardest by the economic reforms, and it has had the most difficulty recovering. In general, the investment coefficient of this sector fell, and although it is slowly increasing in some countries, only in Chile is it showing strong growth, above the average of previous decades. Within this sector, however, there is a great deal of heterogeneity among different types of firms (namely, subsidiaries of transnational corporations, firms belonging to large national conglomerates and small and medium-sized enterprises) and among different branches of individual sectors. The analysis shows why differences in behaviour were so marked after the reforms. The chapter ends with an analysis of each country's industrial performance.

The third chapter looks at the mining and hydrocarbons sectors, for which the central objective of the reforms was to seek and promote foreign investment. Unlike the other sectors, in these two, investment depends on whether there are large reserves that can be exploited economically. Only a few countries meet this criterion, and the study therefore concentrates on them. Moreover, because the products of these sectors are aimed primarily at foreign markets, trends in the world mineral market are one of the main determinants of investment. Institutional changes are thus a necessary element for investment, but they are not sufficient in and of themselves. The institutional reform in these sectors concentrated on guaranteeing higher profits for foreign investment. These changes altered market structure and allowed for new firms and new business strategies, which affected investment.

The fourth chapter covers electricity, telecommunications and highway infrastructure. Profound transformations took place in all three sectors. The infrastructure reform process began with the privatization of public utilities. It was followed by changes in industrial organization and market structure, together with the implementation of new rules of the game, new legislation and new supervisory and regulatory bodies. The participation of private firms and the new institutional environment transformed the logic of investment decisions.

The fifth and final chapter presents the synthesis and conclusions of the study, summing up its contributions to the interpretation of the capital accumulation process during a period of institutional change.

CHAPTER I

INVESTMENT IN A PERIOD OF TRANSITION

The analysis of capital formation presented here focuses on a period when Latin American countries were undergoing changes in their economic institutions, implementing trade and financial liberalization, capital market opening, privatization and labour reforms. This strategy of market liberalization was aimed at integrating the region into the world economy in terms of both trade and finance, deregulating markets and reducing the role of the State as an agent of production, finance and regulation.[8] These changes –whether gradual or abrupt– affected the behaviour of economic actors for a relatively long period of time, which we call the transition period. Our interest is to analyse how those changes affected investment.

A. ECONOMIC REFORMS AND ADAPTATION TO CHANGE

We were able to identify patterns in firms' investment behaviour during the transition period following the reforms. These patterns were repeated in different countries and across a number of sectors, resulting in what we have called investment phases. These phases are closely related to the macroeconomic, political and international context in which the reforms took place.

---

8   See Stallings and Peres (2000) for a general analysis of this process.

1. The Context of the Economic Reforms

An almost universal feature of the period immediately preceding the reforms was economic instability and, in many countries, political instability as well. In Chile, for example, the economic and political crisis unleashed by the Popular Unity government ended in a military coup. In this context, structural changes were imposed abruptly by decree. In Mexico, the foreign debt crisis, which entailed a huge balance-of-payments deficit and thus necessitated adjustments to control inflation, set the scene for reforms. In other cases, such as Argentina, Brazil and Peru, the foreign crisis caused hyperinflation, a phenomenon which also spurred reforms in Bolivia. These countries undertook reforms and a stabilization process simultaneously (see table I-1).

There were two exceptions to this trend of drastic macroeconomic imbalances and major uncertainty leading to a reform process: Colombia and Costa Rica. The relative economic stability of these countries and the gradual manner in which changes were introduced allowed firms to adapt without the pressure of a negative atmosphere.

The countries that launched reforms in the 1990s benefited from the liquidity of the international financial market. There is empirical evidence that adjustment or stabilization policies undertaken when the international situation is unfavourable provoke more intense recessions. This was true, for example, in Chile in 1975, in Bolivia in 1985 and Mexico in 1986.[9] In contrast, the countries that began their reforms in the 1990s benefited from the influx of large amounts of foreign capital, which favoured the expansion of credit and stimulated demand. Consequently, the stabilization programmes came at a lower cost.

Indeed, beginning in 1991, strong capital flows returned. The external interest rate also fell, debt service shrank and the terms of trade stabilized (Moguillansky, 1996). The tremendous increase in foreign direct investment (see table I-2) was identified as a determining factor in investment trends, even though a major part of this investment was concentrated on the purchase of existing assets under the privatization programmes (ECLAC, 1999).

Regardless of the degree of instability prevailing at the time, the investment coefficient (investment as a share of GDP) declined in most countries during the period immediately following the reforms (see figure I-1 and table A-1 in the Annex). The rate of decline and the speed of recovery depended on several factors, such as the degree of firms' uncertainty about institutional changes, the pace of the stabilization effort, the specific manner in which the reform policies and instruments were applied, the coherence of

---

9   See ECLAC, *Economic Survey of Latin America and the Caribbean*, for the corresponding years. In Chile, in 1975, the gross domestic product (GDP) fell by 13% and the terms of trade by 40%; in Bolivia, the GDP dropped by 3% in 1985 and the terms of trade by 6%; in Mexico in 1986, the declines were 4% and 24%, respectively.

Table I-1

ECONOMIC REFORMS AND THE MACROECONOMIC AND INTERNATIONAL CONTEXT

COUNTRY	BEGINNING OF REFORMS	MACROECONOMIC SITUATION	INTERNATIONAL CONTEXT
Argentina	1978 (beginning)	Economic instability	Financial liquidity
	1981-1989 (suspension)	High inflation	
	1991 (resumption)	Stabilization programme (previous hyperinflation: 4,924% in 1989)	Financial liquidity Slight improvement in terms of trade
Bolivia	1985	Stabilization programme (previous hyperinflation: 11,750% in 1985)	Financial Illiquidity Sharp decline in terms of trade
Brazil	1990 (beginning)	Successive failure of stabilization programmes	Financial liquidity
	1994 (new phase)	Real Plan: price stabilization (1994)	Decline in terms of trade
Chile	1974 (beginning)	Stabilization programme (previous hyperinflation: 559% in 1973)	Financial liquidity Decline in terms of trade
	1982-1985 (crisis in model)	Adjustment and stabilization programme	Financial Illiquidity
	1986 (new reform phase)	Stability	Improved terms of trade
Colombia	1990	Stability	Financial liquidity
		Reform preceded by sharp devaluations	Decline in terms of trade

Table I-1 continued

COUNTRY	BEGINNING OF REFORMS	MACROECONOMIC SITUATION	INTERNATIONAL CONTEXT
Costa Rica	1986	Stability	Financial illiquidity Sharp decline in terms of trade
Mexico	1986	High inflation Stabilization programme	Financial illiquidity Sharp decline in terms of trade
Peru	1990	Stabilization programme (previous hyperinflation: 7,482% in 1990)	Financial liquidity Decline in terms of trade

Source: Authors' compilation from the database of the research project.

Table I-2
FOREIGN DIRECT INVESTMENT, 1980-1998
(annual average, millions of dollars)

COUNTRY	1980-1981	1982-1984	1985-1989	1990-1994	1995-1998
Argentina	866	236	730	2 908	5 490
Bolivia	61	15	25	96	583
Brazil	1 929	1 836	1 166	1 035	15 778
Chile	298	201	714	832	3 472
Colombia	140	471	531	763	3 345
Costa Rica	57	45	83	218	448
Jamaica	8	-7	17	122	218
Mexico	2 584	1 878	2 000	5 409	10 426
Peru	76	-1	28	785	2 313
Total	6 018	4 673	5 294	12 167	42 071

Source: Authors' compilation from the database of the Unit on Investment and Corporate Strategies in the ECLAC Division of Production, Productivity and Management.

the signals sent by these policies and instruments with respect to investment, and the international context in which the process evolved. This series of factors resulted in an extremely long period of low investment in some countries. In Chile, for example, it lasted more than a decade, from 1974 to 1985; in Mexico and Bolivia it lasted from 1986 to 1990. In other countries, in contrast, it was brief. In Argentina, in particular, after a long period of declining investment and economic stagnation, there was a positive reaction during the year after the reforms were launched, once hyperinflation was under control.

2. Phases of Post-Reform Investment

The distinction between the initial period of falling investment[10] and the ensuing recovery period gives rise to what we call the phases of firm behaviour during the transition period (see table I-3). These phases coincide with the observed responses not only in the industrial sector, but in all markets that were opened up to national and international competition. Each phase is characterized by one of two identifiable behaviours within a firm: the first

---

10   Part of this decline corresponds to trends in public investment. Unfortunately, the national accounts of the countries under consideration do not have data on public investment. Nevertheless, the deterioration of public-sector capital spending, as reflected in the fiscal accounts, provides important information (see table A-6 in the Annex). The fall in this spending does not, however, account for the total reduction in gross fixed capital formation, which indicates that private investment also fell. This is corroborated by microeconomic information on private firms presented in the chapters on the individual sectors.

Figure I-1
GROSS FIXED CAPITAL FORMATION AS A PERCENTAGE OF GDP

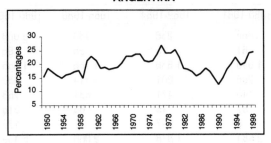

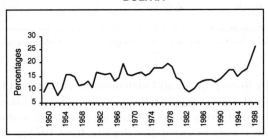

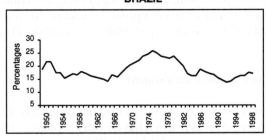

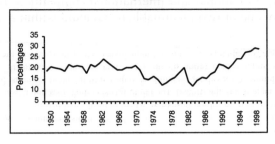

Figure I-1 continued

COLOMBIA

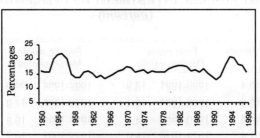

COSTA RICA

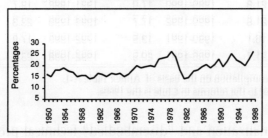

MEXICO

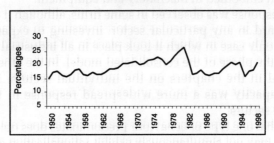

PERU

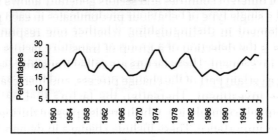

Source: Annex Table A-1.

Table I-3
INVESTMENT PHASES: INVESTMENT AS PERCENTAGE OF GDP
(*percent*)

COUNTRY	PRE-REFORM	FIRST PHASE: RATIONALIZATION		SECOND PHASE: MODERNIZATION		CONSOLIDATED MODEL	
Argentina	23.4	1990-1991	13.9	1992-1998	20.5		
Bolivia	16.9	1986-1989	13.4	1990-1998	17.9		
Brazil	23.3	1990-1993	14.5	1995-1998	16.8		
Chile[a/]	21.4	1974-1976	14.6	1977-1981	16.7		
		1982-1985	14.2	1986-1989	18.3	1990-1998	25.1
Mexico	21.8	1986-1990	17.0	1991-1998[b/]	19.7		
Peru	21.8	1990-1992	17.7	1993-1998	23.3		
Colombia	16.1	1990-1991	13.5	1992-1998	17.8		
Costa Rica	21.7	1986-1991	20.5	1992-1998	23.2		

Source: Authors' compilation on the basis of Annex Table A-1.
a/ The period prior to the reforms in Chile is the 1960s.
b/ Excludes 1995.

features rationalization and "disembodied" technical progress (that is, modernization of business management), and the second is based on modernization embodied in machinery and equipment.

A third response was observed in some firms, although it did not appear across the board in any particular sector: investing to expand production capacity. The only case in which it took place in all industrial sectors was in Chile during the phase of the consolidated model. In the other countries, as demonstrated in the chapters on the individual sectors, investment in expanding capacity was a more widespread response in the privatized infrastructure sectors.

The fact that one type of behaviour predominates does not mean that one firm or sector may not simultaneously exhibit rationalization and investment in modernization, or modernization and expansion, or even all three at once. The analysis of different countries and sectors generally allows us to conclude, however, that a single type of behaviour predominates in each phase.

A key element in distinguishing whether one response or another predominates is the detection of a group of transitory factors stimulating or discouraging investment. These factors are called transitory because they are active during a certain part of the change process, and then cease to stimulate or discourage investment. Thereafter, the factors that have historically determined capital accumulation, which are also present during the transition, take on greater importance. These include changes in demand, variations in relative prices or the cost of capital, technological development and market strategies.

a.   First Phase: Decline in Investment

The first phase is characterized by the strong impact of transitory factors that discourage investment. We have identified two of these:

- *Caution in decision-making*: Given the uncertainty created by all of the institutional and political changes undertaken to cope with macroeconomic instability, the period immediately following the reforms was marked by heightened caution. Firms tended to investigate the economic and political environment, the sustainability of the reforms, trends in relative prices and the behaviour of internal and external competitors, all of which resulted in passive observation and restrained the investment process.
- *Rationalization of production*: Before investing, firms tended to rationalize their operations, lay off employees and introduce new management techniques as an initial defensive move to deal with the opening of the market and imports. This is particularly true of the industrial sector, as well as other sectors of production that are opened up to competition (e.g., energy, mining, infrastructure). It also occurred in privatized enterprises as they attempted to give productivity a quick boost.

In addition to these factors, which are related to the reaction to a new climate of uncertainty, the macroeconomic context provided a disincentive for investment. Table I-4 sums up the principal components of this context, which are also key factors in investment.

Financial liberalization and the lack of bank regulation, together with the monetary contraction required in the stabilization process, produced a domestic interest rate which, when corrected for the exchange rate variation, proved to be grossly out of line with the international interest rate, often resulting in a crisis (see box I-1).

At the same time, the reduction in public spending moderated economic growth rates or generated a recession, although the averages often hid this fact. For example, during the 1974-1985 period, which we have defined as the first phase in Chile, GDP grew at an average rate of 4.4% in the first seven years. That average rate, however, conceals the fact that in 1975, right after the reforms began, GDP plunged 12% in a climate of great instability. GDP rallied later on, only to plummet again in 1982 by 14%. In Argentina in 1990, with the reforms already under way, GDP dipped 1.9%, after a 7% decline the year before. As a result, the average growth of nearly 5% shown in table I-4 actually represents a recovery from previous years' losses.

One consequence of recession is that it aggravates the underutilization of productive capacity, which curbs investment even more sharply. In almost all these countries, opening up the economy coincided with a period of revaluation of the local currency, which diminished the possibility of protecting the industrial sector's markets. Table I-4 shows that revaluation was

Table I-4
FUNDAMENTAL MACROECONOMIC VARIABLES
(percent)

Country	Years	GDP growth rate (average annual variation)	Use of installed capacity (annual average)	Variation in price of capital goods[a]	Gap between domestic and international interest rates[b]	Variation in real exchange rate for the period[c]	Highest inflation rate of the period
		FIRST POST–REFORM PHASE					
Argentina	1990-1991	4.7	50.5	-11.0	100.0	-29.0	1 344
Bolivia	1986-1989	1.7	n.a.	22.4	n.a.	7.9	8 171
Brazil	1990-1993	0.3	72.6	2.9	247.6	-19.5	2 489
Chile	1974-1981	4.4	n.a.	-13.9	26.7	-45.1	375
Chile	1982-1985	-1.3	n.a.	7.8	-10.8	60.1	26
Colombia	1990-1991	2.7	73.1	-4.6	1.7	1.0	32
Costa Rica	1986-1991	4.2	n.a.	4.5	n.a.	9.7	27
Mexico	1986-1990	1.6	n.a.	-11.5	18.3	-38.2	159
Peru	1990-1993	0.6	51.4	-16.4	148.5	-6.9	7 649
		SECOND POST–REFORM PHASE					
Argentina	1992-1998	5.3	70.0	-8.8	14.8	-6.1	17.6
Bolivia	1990-1998	4.3	n.a.	3.9	n.a.	3.9	18.0
Brazil	1995-1998	2.9	78.8	-12.3	48.5	-14.1	22.0
Chile	1986-1989	6.9	n.a.	-3.7	3.0	6.5	21.5
Chile[d]	1990-1998	6.9	80.4	-19.2	10.7	-17.6	27.3
Colombia	1992-1998	3.5	74.4	-22.4	19.9	-22.8	25.1
Costa Rica	1992-1998	4.3	n.a.	-10.2	n.a.	-17.6	22.6
Mexico	1991-1998	3.1	n.a.	3.9	7.8	3.4	18.9
Peru	1994-1998	6.6	70.0	-8.5	23.2	0.3	15.4

Source: Authors' compilation from the database of ECLAC's Economic Development Division.
a/ Variation of the gross capital formation deflator with respect to the GDP deflator, from the beginning of the period to the end of the period.
b/ Calculated as the difference between the domestic nominal rate (i), deflated by the devaluation rate (e), and the London Inter-Bank Offered Rate (LIBOR): [((1+i)/(1+e)-1) – LIBOR].
c/ Last year in period compared to first year; a decline means appreciation of the local currency.
d/ Corresponds to a phase of the consolidated model.

particularly pronounced in Argentina, Brazil (after 1988), Chile (between 1974 and 1981) and Mexico.

The initial response to economic reforms was to rationalize business management and production processes, which we identified as a key factor in this phase. In larger firms, the result was a massive layoff of employees,

Box I-1
MACROECONOMIC POLICY, FINANCIAL LIBERALIZATION, CAPITAL MARKET OPENING AND CRISIS IN LATIN AMERICA

Capital market opening, a policy intended to promote foreign investment and reduce external restrictions, has been one of the most controversial reforms. Theoretically, opening the market stimulates the flow of capital and the availability of one of the scarcest resources in Latin American countries, namely, foreign exchange. In recent decades, however, the main characteristic of these flows has been their volatility.

In the context of macroeconomic policies for stabilizing prices through an exchange rate anchor, governments tended to control spending through monetary policies that drove up interest rates, thus creating a vicious circle that encouraged the entry of short-term foreign capital, accelerated the decline of the real exchange rate, hampered exports and stimulated imports while depressing investment.

This process led to profound financial crises and balance-of-payments problems when the flows changed direction in response to some internal or external stimulus. To avoid future repetitions of this scenario, one group of economists proposes controlling the capital market with different types of instruments (see Ffrench-Davis and Griffith-Jones, 1995; Ffrench-Davis and Reisen, 1998; and Ocampo, 1999). Another group maintains, in contrast, that the most efficient alternative is the complete "dollarization" of economies (see Hausman and others, 1999). This difference of opinion has not yet been resolved.

FINANCIAL CRISES

COUNTRY	PERIOD	MACROECONOMIC CONDITIONS	FINANCIAL PROBLEMS
Argentina	1974-1981	Budget deficit and high inflation; stabilization based on exchange-rate anchor (1978-1981)	Banking crisis
	1995	Sharp adjustment and macroeconomic rigidity due to convertibility law	Banking crisis
Bolivia	1985-1990	Stabilization and structural adjustment after large budget deficits and hyperinflation	Isolated bank failures
Brazil	1995	Stabilization plan with exchange rate anchor; large current-account deficit	Liquidity and solvency problems in the banking industry
Chile	1974-1982	Structural reforms and financial adjustment in the public sector; heavy foreign debt; stabilization based on exchange rate anchor (1978-1982)	Widespread banking crisis
Mexico	1995	Increased inflation, fiscal and monetary adjustment programme to deal with economic crisis unleashed in late 1994	Widespread crisis in the financial system
Peru	1990-1992	Stabilization and structural adjustment after large budget deficits and hyperinflation	Solvency problems in banking industry

Source: Compiled by the authors on the basis of Günter Held, "Bank regulation, liberalization and financial instability in Latin American and Caribbean countries", *Finance and the Real Economy: Issues and Case Studies in Developing Countries*, Yilmaz Akyüz and Günter Held (eds.), Santiago, Chile, Economic Commission for Latin America and the Caribbean (ECLAC) and World Institute of Development Economics Research (WIDER), 1993; Günter Held, "Liberalization or financial development?", *CEPAL Review*, No. 54 (LC/G.1845-P), Santiago, Chile, December 1994; and Economic Commission for Latin America and the Caribbean (ECLAC), *Strengthening Development: The Interplay of Macro- and Microeconomics*, Libros de la CEPAL series, No. 42 (LC/G.1898/Rev.1-P), Santiago, Chile, March 1996. United Nations Publication, sales No. E.96.II.G.2.

which was exacerbated by the failure of small and medium-sized businesses and the restructuring of subsidiaries of transnational and public enterprises. The rationalization process tended to be faster and more intense when the economy was liberalized against a backdrop of severe recession, as happened in Argentina and Chile in the 1970s, Mexico in the early 1980s and Brazil in the early 1990s.

During this initial phase, the capacity to react by boosting exports was generally low in countries whose capital markets had not yet been modernized. In these cases, production processes and machinery were obsolete, and the resulting products could not compete in foreign markets. This was true in several industrial sectors of Peru and Chile when the reforms were implemented. Only in a few exceptional cases were specific industries operating in competitive markets able to quickly reorient their production to the foreign market.

b. Second Phase: Increased Investment in Modernization

In this second phase, the transitory factors primarily stimulated investment and were associated with the emergence of various phenomena:

- *Cost-cutting modernization:* The need to update equipment and machinery is of particular importance after a firm has gone through a period of rationalization and wants to enhance its competitiveness to survive in the market. This is a defensive effort linked to the opening of the economy and the emergence of new actors (firms that import and those that produce) in the same sector.
- *Reorientation towards exports:* Market liberalization and new relative prices created a special stimulus for investment in export sectors in some countries. At the same time, however, there was a wave of destruction, which we could call "disinvestment", which was not reflected in aggregate investment statistics. This trend went hand in hand with an exceptional rise in the import coefficient. Because it is very difficult to measure the latter phenomenon, we cannot calculate the net effects of the new allocation of resources to exports versus imports.
- *Strategic repositioning of transnational firms:* The opening of new markets led to an increased role for transnational corporations, which were able to take advantage of their larger size and the appearance of potential markets in new countries. In addition, prospects for higher profits emerged, especially in sectors in which firms were privatized. This was true not only in industrial sectors, but also in basic infrastructure services –telecommunications, electricity, water and sanitation– and in the oil and gas sectors, where net investment rose sharply as a result of both the acquisition and the expansion of productive capacity.

- *Investments required by privatization contracts:* This phenomenon occurred in countries that imposed as a condition of privatization the expansion of services –particularly in the telecommunications sector– or new investments. For example, investment commitments were required in Peru, and the "capitalization" of enterprises was a condition in Bolivia.[11]

These temporary factors tend to provide a one-time stimulus to investment or, in some cases, for as long as the stimulus for change lasts. The tendency dissipates in the long run, however, when the new economic model takes hold.

Following the initial step of adjusting business management, firms were faced with a macroeconomic context of less uncertainty, a clear trend towards price stability, higher growth in demand, increased utilization of installed capacity and in general less instability of different variables, especially those that are key determinants of the profitability of investment projects. Consequently, the capital accumulation effort picked up steam. Positive factors came to predominate, even though in some countries various macroeconomic imbalances persisted and contributed to great uncertainty throughout the process –albeit to a lesser extent than in the previous phase.

Table I-4 shows that in the second phase GDP grew at an average annual rate ranging from nearly 3% in Brazil and Mexico to nearly 7% in Chile. In five of the eight countries, there was a sharp revaluation of the local currency, which helped bring down the cost of capital goods. The average annual rate of inflation was much lower than in the preceding phase, while the cost of internal financing followed different trajectories in different countries. The gap between the domestic and international interest rates ranged from just 3% in Chile between 1986 and 1989 to 48% in Brazil between 1995 and 1998. Obviously, this is an element that hindered investment in some countries.

Investment in modernization had a high marginal yield in countries where instability had long been an obstacle to healthy investment. This can be explained by at least three factors. First, the relative technological obsolescence of existing capital goods meant that investment in modernization quickly increased average productivity. Second, investment in modernization occurred after the rationalization phase, which prepared businesses to make efficient investment decisions and maximize their technical and operational yields. Third, economic liberalization tended to lower the price of capital goods, a trend which gathered momentum in the 1990s as currencies appreciated.

The high yield resulting from modernizing machinery and equipment explains the increase in investment despite the high real interest rate that

---

11 In Bolivia, the State contributed the public enterprise and the national or foreign investor contributed the capital, in an amount equal to the market value of the public enterprise. This created a new company with twice the value, in which the investor held 50% of the shares and controlled the management of the business, while the remaining shares were distributed to the citizens either directly or by means of the reformed pension fund system.

persisted in some countries (especially Brazil), and despite the microeconomic uncertainties and the consequent need to make drastic changes in growth strategies.[12] Investment during this phase may also take place under adverse circumstances, because the need to lower costs to deal with competition cannot be put off.

It is interesting to note that the main components of gross fixed capital formation –represented by machinery and equipment and by construction (see table I-5)– show the same trends; both rise or fall in consonance with overall gross capital formation during the periods examined. Contrasts among

Table I-5
COMPONENTS AND COEFFICIENT OF GROSS FIXED CAPITAL FORMATION AS A PERCENTAGE OF GDP
(percent)

COUNTRY	1970-1980	1990-1998	1970	1975	1980	1986	1990	1998
MACHINERY AND EQUIPMENT								
Argentina	6.8	7.8	6.3	5.9	8.1	7.3	6.0	9.6
Bolivia	8.8	9.0	7.7	9.2	8.2	5.7	6.1	15.2
Brazil	9.8	5.2	8.6	11.7	9.0	6.4	4.6	6.3
Chile	6.3	10.6	7.3	5.8	8.6	4.6	8.0	13.0
Colombia	6.8	8.6	6.9	6.2	7.7	6.1	6.7	8.1
Costa Rica	10.0	12.6	8.2	8.9	10.2	9.0	12.7	15.3
Mexico	9.0	8.7	8.4	9.8	10.9	5.9	8.0	10.7
Peru	10.4	4.5	7.7	14.9	10.9	5.5	3.8	5.0
CONSTRUCTION								
Argentina	16.6	11.8	16.5	15.3	17.0	9.2	6.7	14.9
Bolivia	8.2	9.0	7.5	-9.0	6.0	7.7	7.8	11.3
Brazil	13.6	10.4	12.0	14.1	14.6	12.3	11.0	10.6
Chile	9.9	14.5	14.3	9.0	10.0	10.7	13.6	15.9
Colombia	9.4	8.3	10.5	9.1	9.1	10.1	7.4	7.4
Costa Rica	11.7	10.2	10.2	10.8	13.7	10.5	10.4	11.5
Mexico	12.8	10.3	12.7	13.1	13.9	10.5	10.4	10.0
Peru	11.4	17.0	9.1	12.6	12.6	11.8	13.6	20.1

Source: Annex tables A-2 and A-3.

---

12 See Kosacoff (1998) and Bielschowsky (1999a).

countries can be seen, however. In the 1990s, the investment coefficient in machinery and equipment fell in Brazil, Mexico and Peru in comparison with historic levels, while in Chile, Colombia and Costa Rica it rose significantly. As the next section shows, this rise was a function of the increased dynamism of the production sectors. Furthermore, average annual investment in construction jumped sharply in Chile and Peru, and in 1998 this sector's share in the GDP expanded considerably in Argentina, as well.

3. Consolidation of the Economic Model

We define the consolidation phase as one in which the temporary incentives for investment have disappeared, and therefore the peculiar elements of the transition period are no longer key determinants of investment. The new institutionality has matured, and investment now depends on factors that are recognized as the determinants in business cycles in normal times.

This phase has not occurred in most of the countries under study; several more years will be required for the processes to mature and the investment environment to become consolidated. Depending on macroeconomic and institutional factors and the entrepreneurial spirit of the actors, investment could either became more or less dynamic in this new period. There is no guarantee that the new set of signals will be able to solve the risk-return equation in such a way as to encourage investment in expanding capacity beyond the achievements of the previous economic model. This is due primarily to the fact that the region still faces a situation of instability, characterized by the following factors:

a) *Great vulnerability:* The globalization of finance and the fact that economies have no protection against the volatility of international capital flows or the fragility of the regional financial system create an atmosphere of vulnerability. These factors do not create a macroeconomic context that favours productive investment in expanding capacity, when such investment is irreversible.

b) *Lower profits, higher risks:* Before the macroeconomic instability that resulted from the debt crisis of the 1980s, investments in tradable goods yielded high profits –albeit thanks to protection in many cases– in a microeconomic context of less uncertainty, and with capital costs that were negative in real terms. The economic reforms created an open, universal microeconomic institutionality without protection and with greater risks. National firms responded by concentrating investment in sectors with very high profits.

c) *Less public investment in infrastructure:* Historically, the public sector invested in basic services in order to create positive externalities. The privatization of these sectors was accompanied by greater demands for profitability, the incorporation of risk costs and an aversion to macroeconomic and microeconomic uncertainty. If the State does not intervene to offset these factors, there is no reason to expect investment to be higher than in the past, especially in energy sectors (electricity and hydrocarbons), highway infrastructure, water and sanitation.

d) *New firms and business strategies:* This could be the most positive development for the future. After abandoning the region throughout the 1970s and 1980s, foreign direct investment returned in the 1990s, attracted by the stabilization of the Latin American economies and the liberalization and deregulation of markets. The question that arises is whether this movement will spur a new cycle of investment in new sectors and new areas of business. So far, there are good signs in certain infrastructure sectors, but they have not spread to the productive sectors.

Chile is the only country that has reached this stage of model consolidation. Since 1990, investment has been more dynamic there than it was in the decades preceding 1970. It is interesting to study the reasons behind this new stage in Chile. As explained in box I-2, the State played a much more important role in this process than is normally acknowledged. On the other hand, this vigour could dissipate in the future if the proper policies are not maintained (Moguillansky, 1999).

In three countries, nearly 15 years have passed since the reforms were launched, and the model has not yet been consolidated. The transitory factors typical of a process of change are still having a tremendous impact on investment decisions. In Bolivia, at the end of the 1990s investment behaviour was still strongly influenced by the ongoing capitalization of formerly public enterprises; in Costa Rica, the reforms have been implemented gradually, and they are now in a phase of strong investment resulting from the continued repositioning of transnational corporations; and in Mexico, an ongoing trend toward the reallocation of resources was prompted by the entry of United States firms, stimulated by the North American Free Trade Agreement (NAFTA) and the opening of a huge market thanks to the integration process, coupled with the devaluation following the 1994 crisis. Finally, in Argentina, Brazil, Colombia and Peru, the reforms have been in place less than 10 years and the transition is still under way, so the new institutional structure has not yet taken root.

Box I-2
THE ROLE OF THE STATE IN THE CONSOLIDATION
OF THE ECONOMIC MODEL IN CHILE

Chile began its economic reforms 25 years ago, undergoing at that time the process that the other countries in the region are experiencing now. In the transition period characterized by economic orthodoxy, we can identify an initial phase dominated by a number of negative signals stemming from the interaction of policies and reforms that led to unsatisfactory investment behaviour. This phase, which began in 1974, culminated in a severe economic crisis, catalysed by the impact of external events in 1982.

In order to overcome the economic crisis and help private industry recover, the military regime supported and stimulated productive activity, assuming debts and losses and granting subsidies. As a result, large amounts of money were transferred from the public to the private sector.

Beginning in 1985, the State employed a variety of mechanisms as it continued to intervene to strengthen private industry:

- It regulated financial markets, providing agents with a strict framework of rules and penalizing the misuse of resources.
- It intervened to reincorporate the private sector into production, generating stimuli with new and creative instruments, including reduced share prices in enterprises and banks that were transferred to the private sector after going bankrupt, special credits and the privatization of public utilities through the mechanism of "popular capitalism" (thanks to this formula, public officials and executives of State enterprises and economic groups were able to obtain controlling interest in privatized companies).
- It intervened to create new stimuli for foreign investment (Chapter XIX of the Central Bank's Compendium of Standards for International Change).
- It intervened to expand the financial market, establishing mechanisms to allow for part of the resources accumulated by pension fund administrators (long-term resources) to be used as a source of investment financing.
- It applied a series of incentives to promote exports, which, together with the policy of favouring a low value for the local currency that would remain stable in the medium term, generated the profits required for the diversification of exports into non-traditional areas.

The "dirigisme" in public policy that characterized the second phase paved the way for the restructuring of economic groups, the emergence of new domestic and foreign firms, the modernization of production in industries processing natural resources and an orientation towards competing in foreign markets.

The post-reform transition period ended in early 1990, giving way to the consolidation of the economic model. There was a strong surge in investment during this period, which can be explained by four elements: positive macroeconomic trends, expansion of the capital market, a favourable international context and the dynamic that had characterized sectors

Box I-2 continued

making intensive use of natural resources and various infrastructure sectors since the late 1980s as they forged ahead without obstacles to development.

In the second half of the 1990s, however, as the economic model matured, a fourth phase began to take shape. It marks the culmination of a business cycle resulting from the declining yields of capital in activities where investment had been concentrated in the last decade, the disappearance of the major incentives provided by the State, the fall in international prices for some products that had become principal exports and the extension of market regulation or the implementation of stricter regulations.

Source: Compiled by the authors on the basis of Graciela Moguillansky, *La inversión en Chile: ¿el fin de un ciclo de expansión?*, Santiago, Chile, Economic Commission for Latin America and the Caribbean (ECLAC)/Fondo de Cultura Económica, 1999.

B. TRANSITORY FACTORS IN SECTORAL INVESTMENT

The research project that resulted in this book made it possible to compile statistics for various countries showing the development of sector-level investment in the period following the reforms. This, in turn, enabled us to make a comparison with a previous period, which would be as long as possible. The latter exercise was limited by the lack of information, as figures dated back only to 1970 in most cases or, exceptionally, to the 1960s.[13]

1. What the Sectoral Data Show

Table I-6 shows data for the sectors that we believe are essential to sustained growth over the long term. These sectors are divided into two groups: the first includes industry, mining and hydrocarbons, and the second includes electricity, telecommunications and transportation. The first group is characterized by the generation or savings of foreign exchange, so its

---

13   With respect to Argentina and Mexico, it was not possible to construct a full data matrix because of the lack of historical data in some cases, or because only very partial information was available. In these countries, therefore, the analysis focused on each sector individually.

Table I-6
SECTORAL INVESTMENT COEFFICIENTS
(annual average for the period, as percent of overall GDP)

COUNTRY/SECTOR	PRE-REFORM	POST-REFORM		
BOLIVIA		1987-1989	1990-1995	1996-1997
Production sectors	n.a.	5.11	6.13	6.23
Hydrocarbons		3.40	3.90	4.06
Industry		1.40	1.49	1.40
Mining		0.31	0.74	0.77
Infrastructure sectors		1.56	2.35	3.81
Electricity		0.83	1.53	2.16
Sanitation		0.32	0.15	0.23
Telecommunications		0.41	0.67	1.42
BRAZIL	1970-1989	1990-1994	1995-1997	
Production sectors	5.05	2.60	3.80	
Hydrocarbons	0.95	0.50	0.40	
Industry	3.90	2.00	3.30	
Mining	0.20	0.10	0.10	
Infrastructure sectors	4.58	2.34	2.18	
Electricity	1.83	0.91	0.55	
Sanitation	0.35	0.19	0.13	
Telecommunications	0.62	0.49	0.70	
Transportation	1.78	0.75	0.80	
CHILE		1980-1985	1986-1989	1990-1997
Production sectors	n.a.	5.18	6.32	8.98
Hydrocarbons		0.93	0.80	0.81
Industry		1.87	2.31	3.81
Mining		2.38	3.21	4.36
Infrastructure sectors		4.68	4.14	5.59
Electricity		1.82	1.56	1.52
Sanitation, roads, ports		1.47	1.15	1.71
Telecommunications		0.47	0.68	1.50
Others		0.92	0.75	0.86

Table I-6 continued

COUNTRY/SECTOR	PRE-REFORM		POST-REFORM	
COLOMBIA	1975-1989	1990-1991	1992-1995	1996-1997
Production sectors	3.33	3.30	4.69	n.a.
Hydrocarbons	0.96	1.05	2.22	2.96
Industry	2.37	2.25	2.47	n.a.
Infrastructure sectors	4.04	3.52	5.84	6.52
Water and sanitation	0.30	0.35	0.60	0.70
Communications	0.37	0.40	0.71	1.61
Electricity	1.95	1.68	2.45	2.73
Transportation	1.42	1.09	2.08	1.48
COSTA RICA	1970-1985	1986-1991	1992-1994	
Production sectors	5.89	7.36	8.26	
Agriculture	1.75	2.45	2.82	
Industry	4.14	4.91	5.44	
Infrastructure sectors	5.71	5.87	7.79	
Electricity	1.90	1.83	2.60	
Transportation	3.81	4.04	5.19	
PERU	1970-1989	1992-1993	1994-1997	
Production sectors	7.99	4.18	4.79	
Agriculture	0.38	0.75	0.79	
Hydrocarbons	0.74	0.21	0.22	
Industry	4.84	2.23	2.84	
Mining	2.03	0.99	0.94	
Infrastructure sectors	3.94	3.48	3.84	
Electricity and water	0.81	1.14	1.24	
Transportation and communications	3.13	2.34	2.60	

Source: Authors' compilation from the database of the research project. Note: The coefficients are expressed in constant currency of each country. The figures of the various countries are not comparable with each other.

expansion prevents recurring crises in the balance of payments and external limitations on growth; the sectors in the second group are characterized by their contribution to strong international competitiveness, and they are fundamental to the growth of the first group.

The first significant result in the sectors that produce goods (the first group) is that in the period following the reforms, capital was channelled preferentially to sectors exporting primary goods, while investment in the industrial sector declined. This is consistent with the general tendency for the gross industrial product's share of the overall GDP to gradually shrink. In only two countries did investment in the industrial sector rise, as measured by the coefficient of investment with respect to GDP: Chile and Costa Rica. This result also explains the small proportion of manufactured goods in exports, which continues to characterize in the region's export sector, with the exception of Mexico and Brazil. Moreover, the weakness of investments in the industrial sector in the latter two countries demonstrates the vulnerability of the export sector when looking toward the future.

According to a survey conducted in Argentina, investment had recovered in a small group of industrial branches by 1996. The same can be seen in an industrial survey carried out in Brazil between 1995 and 1997, but in this case the investment coefficient was lower than that registered prior to the reforms. In Peru, the figures compiled by the National Institute of Statistics and Computing (INEI) show that by 1997 the industrial sector as a whole was still far from regaining the levels of investment of the period preceding the reforms.

In the mining and hydrocarbons sectors, Chile and Colombia stand out for the dynamic nature of investment. In addition, as is discussed in the corresponding chapter, the country-by-country sectoral studies indicate that investment projects in mining are being considered in Argentina and Peru, and projects are also being evaluated in different segments of the petroleum and gas industry. The prospects for these sectors appear to be favourable in countries where the effects of incentives for foreign investment are maturing.

With the exception of Brazil and Peru, investment in infrastructure rose sharply after the reforms were implemented, in comparison with the 1980s; such investment also increased its share of GDP. Unlike Argentina and Chile, where the private sector has played a major role in sectoral growth, in Colombia and Costa Rica the public sector has led the accumulation effort in infrastructure to date. In the other countries, it is too early to draw a definite conclusion about the future behaviour of private firms. In the respective chapters, however, sectoral and microeconomic factors that could hinder the future development of investment are discussed.

2.   *Transitory Factors as Determinants of Sectoral Investment*

Table I-7 analyses the performance of the different sectors in the 1990s, classifying them as highly dynamic, moderately dynamic, or non-dynamic and comparing production and service activities in the different countries. Some noteworthy points are as follows:

a)   The country-by-country analysis reveals that all sectors in Chile were highly dynamic, whereas investment in Brazil followed a negative trend in most sectors. This indicates that as the liberalization model took root in Chile, the private sector adopted a general pro-expansion attitude

Table I-7
DYNAMIC SECTORS IN THE 1990s

COUNTRY	INDUSTRY	MINING	PETROLEUM	TELECOMMUNICATIONS	ENERGY	TRANSPORTATION
Chile	H	H	n.a.	H	H	H
Argentina	M	M/H	H	H	M/H	M
Colombia	M	n.a.	H	H	M	N
Bolivia	N	M	M	H	H	n.a.
Peru	N	M/H	N	H	M	H
Mexico	M	n.a	N/M	H	M	H
Brazil	M	N	N	H	N	N

Source: Authors' compilation from the database of the research project.
H = highly dynamic; M = moderately dynamic; N = non-dynamic.

(although as shown below, this is not true across the board in all companies or in all subsectors; the most dynamic firms raise the investment average). In Brazil, on the other hand, the difficulty in achieving stabilization and the turbulence that characterized the initial post-reform transition period dampened investment in the 1990s. The remaining countries reveal heterogeneous situations across sectors, as some benefited and others suffered.

b)   In the sector-by-sector analysis, telecommunications appears to have been the most dynamic, followed by energy and transportation, while the performance of production sectors was much more moderate. In the infrastructure sectors, investment was favoured by transitory factors, which are examined in detail in the respective chapters. In mining and petroleum, the transformations occurred too recently to reach a conclusion, given that the time between exploration, the beginning of feasibility studies and actual mining or drilling is quite long. Finally, as the figures show, industry was among the worst-performing sectors in the period following the reforms.

How dynamic investment was in a given sector can be explained by specific factors. Certain institutional aspects, linked to changes in legal and regulatory frameworks and to the nature of the markets, became particularly important to investment. Many of these aspects were only temporary, however (see table I-8), and as mentioned earlier, they were associated with a number of elements:

Table I-8
TRANSITORY FACTORS STIMULATING INVESTMENT

Country	Special Incentives for Foreign Investment	Investment in Defensive Modernization	Strategic Repositioning of Transnational Firms	Investment and Expansion Commitments After Privatization	Specific Institutional Changes	Investments Stimulated by Regional Integration
INDUSTRY						
Argentina		+	+		+	+
Bolivia		+	+			
Brazil		+	+		+	+
Chile	+	+	+			
Colombia		+	+			
Costa Rica	+	+	+		+	
Mexico		+	+		+	+
Peru		+	+			
MINING						
Argentina	+	+	+	+	+	+
Bolivia	+				+	+
Brazil					+	
Chile	+	+	+			+
Colombia						
Costa Rica					+	
Mexico						
Peru	+	+	+		+	+
HYDROCARBONS						
Argentina	+	+	+		+	+
Bolivia	+	+	+	+	+	+
Brazil			+		+	
Chile						
Colombia	+	+	+			
Costa Rica						+
Mexico					+	+
Peru	+	+	+			
ELECTRICITY						
Argentina		+	+		+	+
Bolivia		+	+	+	+	+
Brazil		+	+		+	+
Chile	+	+	+		+	.
Colombia		+	+		+	
Costa Rica		+			+	+
Mexico		+	+		+	
Peru		+	+	+	+	

Table I-8 continued

Country	Special Incentives for Foreign Investment	Investment in Defensive Modernization	Strategic Repositioning of Transnational Firms	Investment and Expansion Commitments after Privatization	Specific Institutional Changes	Investments Stimulated by Regional Integration
		TELECOMMUNICATIONS				
Argentina		+	+	+	+	
Bolivia		+	+	+	+	
Brazil		+	+	+	+	
Chile	+	+	+	+	+	
Colombia		+	+	+	+	
Costa Rica		+				
Mexico		+	+	+	+	
Peru		+	+	+	+	
		HIGHWAY INFRASTRUCTURE				
Argentina		+		+	+	
Bolivia		+			+	
Brazil		+		+	+	
Chile		+		+	+	
Colombia		+		+	+	
Costa Rica		+				
Mexico		+		+	+	
Peru		+			+	

Source: Authors' compilation from the database of the research project.

a) Defensive modernization (to boost competitiveness) was especially significant in industry, but it was also observed in both private and public enterprises in the mining and hydrocarbons sectors. This kind of modernizing investment, aimed at increasing efficiency and profitability, also occurred in electricity, telecommunications and highway infrastructure.

b) Most industrial branches in which investment grew strongly saw an increase in investment by transnational firms seeking to bolster their strategic share in markets opening up to competition. This is also true of mining and hydrocarbons, where institutional changes allowed the entry of foreign capital, and of electricity and telecommunications after privatization was implemented.

c) Changes in legislation governing mining and hydrocarbons provided an additional stimulus to foreign investment. This also occurred in specific industrial branches (including the automotive industry, textiles and electronics assembly) when incentive mechanisms were introduced or enhanced.

d) The commitment to invest in privatized companies boosted investment, either because stock was sold under the rubric of capitalization, as in the case of Bolivia, or because investment commitments were made, as in the case of Peru. There were also commitments to expand and modernize services, which entailed large investments; this was an especially important factor in telecommunications.

e)   The vigour of investment in telecommunications can be explained by the battle among transnational firms to dominate the world market and the Latin American market in particular, the tremendous pent-up demand for fixed telephone service, the strong development of technology and the backwardness of the existing industry.

f)   In the particular case of Mexico and other Central American and Caribbean countries, a wave of investment was associated with integration with the United States market. Although this trend began before the reforms were launched, they have given it greater impetus. The same occurred in the countries that make up the Southern Common Market (Mercosur).

All of these elements together contributed to the improved investment behaviour that characterized the second phase of the transition to a new economic model. It is not possible, however, to determine how the individual sectors will evolve once the new institutions become entrenched and the transitory incentives disappear.

CHAPTER II

INVESTMENT IN THE INDUSTRIAL SECTOR

A. A DEFENSIVE STANCE IN THE FACE OF CHANGE: A SECTORAL OVERVIEW

The industrial sector was hardest hit by the economic reforms, with a higher cost of adjustment than in any other sector.[14] The investment coefficient for this sector fell, recovered slowly in some countries and only in the case of Chile was able to grow strongly enough to exceed the averages for previous decades. The most drastic changes in the industrial sector were triggered by market opening and liberalization. Interviews with businesspeople and detailed surveys carried out in several countries all lead to the conclusion that entrepreneurs in the industrial sector adopted a defensive position in response to liberalization and deregulation.

1. The First Phase in the Industrial Sector

The simple need to ensure survival forced the industrial sector into rationalization and cost reduction, with no medium-term alternative. The impact on industry of both institutional and macroeconomic change was therefore greater than that on the economy as a whole.

---

14 The information contained in the text, tables, boxes and figures in this chapter is taken from the database of this research. It is the result of work by the following authors: Abugattás (1999); Barja (1999a); Bielschowsky (1999a); Bisang and Gómez (1999); Cordero (2000); Mendiola (1999); Moreno-Brid (1999); Ramirez and Núñez (1999).

Table II-1
THE THREE PHASES OF POST-REFORM INVESTMENT IN INDUSTRY

COUNTRY	PRE-REFORM		PHASE I: INVESTMENT IN RATIONALIZATION			PHASE II: INVESTMENT IN MODERNIZATION			CONSOLIDATION OF THE MODEL		
	PERIOD	SHARE OF ANNUAL AVERAGE GDP %	PERIOD	PRE-REFORM INDEX = 100 a/ PERIOD INDEX	SHARE OF ANNUAL AVERAGE GDP %	PERIOD	PRE-REFORM INDEX = 100 PERIOD AVERAGE	SHARE OF ANNUAL AVERAGE GDP %	PERIOD	PRE-REFORM INDEX = 100 PERIOD AVERAGE	SHARE OF ANNUAL AVERAGE GDP %
Argentina	1970-1990	3.3	1991	100	2.0	1992-1997	166	3.0			
Brazil	1970-1989	3.9	1990-1994	78	2.0	1995-1997	130	3.3			
Chile	1960-1974	n.a.	1974-1985	100	1.4	1986-1989	177	2.3	1990-1997	460	3.8
Colombia	1970-1989	2.3				1990-1995	166	2.3			
Mexico	1970-1985	1.9	1986-1990	67	1.0	1991-1994	118	1.4			
Peru	1970-1989	4.8	1990-1995	37	2.6						

Source: Authors' compilation from the database of the research project.
a/The figure for Chile and Argentina corresponds to the average of phase I = 100.

Key among the institutional changes that affected the sector was the scrapping of tariff and non-tariff barriers in specific branches of industry, as well as the elimination of sectoral policies providing subsidies, tax exemptions and loans at preferential rates. This coincided with the elimination of policies to promote industrial exports. The combined effect of these changes was a disincentive to investment in the industrial sector.

As a consequence, the investment coefficient registered in the countries during the first phase was well below the historical average for the period prior to liberalization. This is confirmed by table II-1, which shows not only lower shares of GDP, but also lower absolute levels compared to those of the pre-reform period.

2. The Second Phase in the Industrial Sector

As mentioned in the previous chapter, the second phase of the post-reform transition took place in an improved macroeconomic climate with stronger incentives to modernize. Three factors combined to foster modernization in the industrial sector: the improvement in the macroeconomic environment; rising inflows of foreign capital (with a growing share of foreign direct investment within these); and the greater availability of domestic loans and finance.

Alongside these factors, others of a more institutional nature played an important role in defining the development of industrial investment in each country. Particularly significant among these were the establishment of export promotion policies; the reassessment of special industrial regimes; the absorption of national firms by transnational corporations; and other policies which, as shown below, contributed to different investment patterns across the numerous industrial sectors.

This second phase featured a generalized recovery of investment in all countries (table II-1). In Chile, although data are not available for the pre-reform period (in this case the 1960s), the strong growth in investment registered between the mid-1980s and the early 1990s is likely to have surpassed that of the 1960s. The other countries in the study grew at a slower pace, although they were approaching the pre-reform periods.

Table II-2
SECTORAL POLICIES IN THE INDUSTRIAL SECTOR

COUNTRY AND PERIOD	SECTORAL POLICY
ARGENTINA	
1978	Existence of special programmes for manufacturing
1990-1998	Elimination of special regimes apart from in the automotive industry
1991-1998	Elimination of subsidies and loans to specific sectors
1991-1992	Elimination of special export incentives
1993-1998	Tariff and tax benefits for export firms
	Intensification of integration with Mercosur
BRAZIL	
1990-1994	Elimination of special export incentives
	Elimination of subsidized resources for investment
1994-1999	Intensification of integration with Mercosur
COLOMBIA	
1990	Elimination of industrial promotion policies
CHILE	
1974-1984	Elimination of export subsidies
	Reform of land and water markets to foster agroindustrial growth
	Reforestation subsidies
1985	Reform of laws regulating pension fund administrators (AFPs) to permit investment in companies
1986-1989	Temporary tariff increases
1985-1995	Export promotion policies
MEXICO	
1986-1990	Elimination of specific programmes except for in automotive industry
	Elimination of subsidies
	Increased tax benefits for assembly plants and their suppliers
1992-1998	Development bank operating like a "second tier bank", but providing few resources to small and medium-sized firms
	Tax promotion schemes for exports
	Special loans for production and import of assembly plant inputs (decree 1994)
PERU	
1990-1998	Elimination of specific industrial development programmes
	Elimination of subsidies

Source: Authors' compilation from the database of the research project.

B. THE VARYING RESPONSES OF FIRMS AND SECTORS

Moving the analysis to the sectoral and firm level demonstrates that neither the incentives themselves nor the entrepreneurs' responses to them were homogeneous. Indeed, the processes of rationalization and modernization acquired their own particular characteristics among the different firms. Firms generally tended to cut costs and improve both product quality and client-supplier relations, which led to efficiency gains and massive unemployment. Other responses differed according to the type of firm.

1. The Reactions of Large Firms

Large firms –both national and transnational– dealt with the institutional changes by restructuring, which in turn led to the specialization of production; the breakdown of linkages in both processes and products, which transformed complex productive processes into simple assembly operations (the emergence of the assembly plant industry in Mexico and Central America is perhaps the most obvious example of this); and an increase in outsourcing within industry (Katz, 1996; Kosacoff, 1998). A number of innovative organizational practices were introduced to increase efficiency ("total quality", "just-in-time", Japan's "kamban" and others) in what has come to be known as "disembodied" technical progress. These transformations allowed large firms, including the subsidiaries of transnational corporations, to adapt to the new competitive environment.

With the economy stabilized, firms began to employ a longer-term planning horizon. In the largest firms this meant taking decisions on several issues, including strategic partnerships with foreign investors; expansion into new markets; alliances with firms in other countries; introduction of new technologies in terms of products, processes and organization; and the sale of the firm to actors better positioned to exploit its particular assets.

Greater access to credit and a stable economic environment combined to create an incentive to modernize and raise both production and productivity. Such behaviour was observed in most industrial branches, although the degree to which it occurred and the type of transformation it produced varied across firms.

Investment was therefore at its most dynamic in large firms, particularly transnational corporations. This was the case not only because these firms started from a more solid competitive and financial position, but also because capital market liberalization provided them with more financing options, and at lower costs. Indeed, the opening of financial markets in a context of strong international liquidity favoured the execution of large investment projects. These projects were financed with new resources provided directly by foreign investors, with the issue of shares and bonds by the largest firms in international markets and with loans from foreign banks at interest rates far lower than those offered by the domestic financial system.

Another group of factors, however, further explains the particularly dynamic investment patterns found among transnationals.

a) These firms face fewer risks and less uncertainty. For national firms, financial risk was concentrated in a single country, whereas transnational corporations diversified their investments across many countries.

b) The features of the oligopolistic markets in which transnational corporations prefer to operate –product markets that are undergoing constant differentiation in Latin America– encouraged long-term investment aimed at acquiring a stronger market position that was to some extent insulated from the short- and medium-term fluctuations of the local economy.

c) The Latin American subsidiaries of transnational corporations suffered less as a result of liberalization than did local enterprises because of the financial solidity of their parent companies, better access to all types of financing and technology and greater experience in competing internationally thanks to their global networks of input sourcing, export distribution and sales. Consequently, they were more flexible than national firms in the face of the new conditions emerging from liberalization.

Studies carried out among the 100 largest industrial companies in Latin America indicate that between 1990 and 1996 transnational corporations increased their relative share among the large private industrial enterprises.[15] ECLAC (1998) shows that in 1997 foreign investors accelerated their acquisition of assets from local private firms, representing 40% of total foreign investment inflows into Latin America. Because this process was concentrated in three countries, the share of such flows was much higher there: 98% in Argentina and 62% in Mexico.

The larger the presence of transnational corporations, the greater the growth of investment. Bisang and Gómez (1999), who surveyed approximately 1,400 firms in Argentina, show that the participation of transnationals in total manufacturing investment exceeded 52% in 1992 and rose to 57% by 1996. Kosacoff and Porta (1997) calculate that the participation of transnationals in

---

15   See Peres (1998) and CEPAL (1998).

the invoicing of Argentina's 500 largest industrial enterprises grew from 33.6% in 1990 to 51% in 1995.[16]

In Brazil, transnational corporations were dominant in four of the six fastest growing industrial branches: automobiles, electric and electronic products, branded processed foods targeted at the domestic market, and hygiene and cleaning products (Bielschowsky, 1999a).

In Mexico, where the sectoral profile of investment growth is similar to that in Brazil, transnationals were responsible for most of the jump in investment. According to a study by Moreno-Brid (1999), the presence of foreign capital is a key feature in most of the fastest growing industrial branches, which were the recipients of significant levels of foreign direct investment. Mexico's assembly (maquila) industry, which is the nucleus of manufacturing growth, is very closely associated with foreign capital.

In Chile, transnational corporations did not represent a dominant share of the fastest growing manufacturing sectors until the mid-1990s, with the exception of food and beverages. However, local economic groups had developed strategic alliances with foreign capital to promote the growth and modernization of production. These alliances, which had until then been restricted to capital contributions with no equity participation, allowed these conglomerates to penetrate foreign markets, to grow and subsequently to develop cross-border production.

2. The Reactions of Small and Medium-Sized Firms

Small and medium-sized firms have been marginal to the process of capital formation in the post-reform period. The share of these enterprises fell not only in gross capital formation but also in production owing to two factors. First, they were not able to compete with cheaper imported products. This phenomenon became widespread in some industrial branches, including textiles, footwear, machine tools. The second factor was the elimination of preferential loans at subsidized interest rates, which had been targeted to small and medium-sized firms. The institutions that provided these loans were closed down during this period, most notably in Argentina, Chile, Mexico and Peru. Because small and medium-sized firms were largely characterized by fragile microeconomic features, low productivity and limited access to financial resources, they were seriously affected by liberalization and constituted a high percentage of total bankruptcies in the market.

---

16 Chudnovsky, López and Porta (1995) refer to a foreign direct investment boom in Argentina following stabilization and, following Dunning's analytical approach, produce an excellent table outlining the different strategies pursued by multinationals in that country over the 1990s. Kosacoff and Porta (1997) return to this theme, updating the information and completing the analysis of strategies in a broad and creative manner.

Once they had taken the first steps in adapting to the reforms, small and medium-sized enterprises benefited from the more stable environment, growth and the indirect demand generated by the most dynamic sectors. Particularly in foodstuffs, large firms demanded specific inputs from small and medium-sized firms, thereby spreading some of their own growth. This allowed them to grow in absolute terms in certain countries (for example, Mexico), although in others their development was hindered by an inability to compete with imported products and by high domestic interest rates.

With only limited access to capital markets, small and medium-sized firms were adversely affected by financial costs that grew fasten than their profits. Mexico maintained some financing targeted specifically to this sector, particularly when the former development bank became a second-tier public financial institution that lent at preferential rates to small and medium-sized firms, export firms and infrastructure projects. In Chile (Moguillansky, 1999) and Peru (Abugattás, 1999), small firms were marginalized from the market in almost all sectors, while in Mexico this occurred in productive activities in which the process of capital concentration became accelerated.

3.   *The Heterogeneity Among Branches of Industry*

A degree of heterogeneity in the effects of the reforms is also evident across the different industrial branches. Studies on the first phase conducted in Chile (Mizala, 1992) and Argentina (Kosacoff, 1998; Bisang and Gómez, 1999) show that in the early years following market liberalization, investment in non-tradable goods was prioritized over that in tradables.

To evaluate the behaviour of investment in the post-reform transition, we developed the concept of "relative dynamism". We calculated historical averages based on the two previous decades wherever the information was available, otherwise using the longest previous period possible. Those segments of manufacturing industry whose participation in aggregate industrial investment in the post-liberalization period surpassed the historical average are then defined as the most dynamic branches within a country.[17] The studies cited, which are the main sources for this analysis, provide a detailed presentation, description and analysis of the evidence on the development of the different branches within each country, disaggregated to three and four digits of the ISIC code.

Table II-3 (which summarizes the table in annex A-7) presents the industrial branches which experienced the most dynamic investment growth,

---

17   Our definition of "relative dynamism" means that some firms registering scarce absolute expansion are included in the branches labelled "more dynamic". By the same token, in those countries registering a greater aggregate dynamism –especially Chile– some branches experiencing a high rate of expansion are included amongst the "least dynamic" ones.

Table II-3
DECLINING SECTORAL GROWTH

BRANCHES ORGANIZED ACCORDING TO "RELATIVE DYNAMISM"[a]	ISIC CODE	COUNTRIES WHERE THE BRANCH HAS BEEN "RELATIVELY" DYNAMIC[a]	MAIN INVESTORS
Food	311	All countries	Transnationals, conglomerates and large national firms
Metal products	381	All countries	Transnationals, conglomerates and large national firms
Pharmaceutical industry/toiletries/other chemical products	352	All countries except Chile	Transnationals
Basic metallurgy	371	All countries except Peru	Large national firms
Other foodstuffs, beverages and tobacco	31 (excluding 311)	Argentina, Colombia, Chile and Mexico	Large national firms and some transnationals
Chemicals/basic petrochemicals	351	Argentina, Chile, Colombia and Peru	Transnationals
Plastics	356	Brazil, Colombia, Chile, Mexico	Medium-sized and large national firms
Other non-metal minerals	369	Chile, Colombia and Mexico	Large national firms
Automotive industry	384	Argentina, Brazil and Mexico	Transnationals
Wood, paper and pulp	341	Colombia, Chile and Peru	Large national firms
Textile industry/ clothing	321-322	Colombia, Peru and Mexico (maquila assembly plants)	Medium-sized and large national firms
Machinery and mechanical and electrical equipment	382-383	-	-

Source: Authors' compilation from the database of the research project.

a/ Criteria of "relative dynamism": increase in share of aggregate post-reform industrial investment, over that in pre-reform period in each country.

ranked by their prevalence in the individual countries. All countries report particularly dynamic rates of investment in foodstuffs and basic metals. At the next level in terms of relative sectoral growth are the activities associated with the pharmaceutical industry, beauty products and other chemical products; basic metallurgy; basic chemicals and petrochemicals; plastics; other non-metallic minerals; automobiles; wood, pulp and paper; machinery and mechanical and electrical equipment and textiles and clothing.

The concentration of investment in certain branches is explained either by characteristics specific to the branch or by the institutional changes that facilitated branch development.

- *Branches with natural comparative advantages:* The economic reforms allowed such activities to develop in some countries, but behaviour among industrial branches was not homogeneous. In the case of foodstuffs, the elimination of price controls was important, together with corrections in relative prices and, in some countries, a new treatment of agriculture (such as the development of the land and water markets which stimulated investment in primary production and thereby generated the conditions for the broader development of agroindustry). In other countries, policies were designed to stimulate primary production; the elimination of controls in industrial fishing; subsidies for forest exploitation (Chile); and the lifting of restrictions on the exploitation of these resources by private and foreign firms (Mexico). All of this was beneficial to the development of industry's potential, particularly within the foodstuffs, wood and pulp branches.

The iron and steel industry and petrochemicals are two other branches with natural comparative advantages. The former was still predominantly State owned in the late 1980s and early 1990s. As the firms were privatized and absorbed into large economic conglomerates, rapid capital accumulation led to modernization and expansion, particularly in Argentina, Brazil and Chile.

In the case of petrochemicals, some countries witnessed great investment growth following privatization. However, capital formation did not rise in those countries where privatization failed to inspire confidence among private actors, or where institutional problems marred the process. This was the case in Brazil and Mexico (Bielschowsky, 1999a; Moreno-Brid, 1999).

- *Branches linked to construction and infrastructure:* These include metal products and basic inputs for civil engineering, such as cement, glass, clay products and other products unlikely to be exported owing to high transport and distribution costs. These products have a high elasticity with respect to domestic demand, and their development therefore depends on local macroeconomic conditions. They benefited from the re-activation and growth of construction in the 1990s and, in some countries, from infrastructure privatizations, which gave rise to strong investment designed to increase capacity.

- *Pharmaceuticals and other chemical products:* Aside from demand growth, these goods benefited from the growth strategies of transnationals, which successfully exploited the new industrial property laws and the elimination of barriers on importing raw materials from parent companies. These firms invested in continuing to produce final goods for the local market, thereby avoiding the importation costs and risks associated with possible technical and hygiene restrictions, while also exploiting the sunk costs in marketing and distribution.

- *The automotive industry:* This branch benefited from sectoral development policies that were maintained during the implementation of reforms or that are currently in transition. It was the best performer in terms of investment in the three largest countries in the region. In Mexico, the three existing North American assembly plants reinforced an investment strategy favouring integration with the United States, a strategy that first emerged in the 1970s and was consolidated in the 1990s under the impetus of the North American Free Trade Association (NAFTA). The strategy in Brazil and Argentina was to increase their share of the wider Mercosur market. It is estimated that the productive capacity of the European and North American firms increased from two to four million vehicles per year, even though the combined market of these two countries is unable to absorb more than two and a half million. Colombia is a different case in the sense that the local assembly plants sought not to increase capacity but rather to guarantee the recovery of their sunk costs –which the other countries accomplished through special protection schemes– by investing in modernization. For obvious reasons associated with market size and economies of scale, Chile saw little investment in its automotive industry, while firms actually closed down in Peru.

- *The electronic industry:* This branch was strengthened in Mexico and Brazil as a result of the growth strategy pursued by the transnational firms operating in these countries. In the case of Mexico, the improvement was directly related to the development of the maquila industry, as well as integration with the United States. In Brazil, the domestic market and Mercosur –which was expanding rapidly in terms of both household and telecommunications equipment– together stimulated modernization, diversification and the local expansion of existing productive activity. In general, however, the fact that transnational corporations dominate global technological development, combined with the absence of both economies of scale and an industrial culture in this type of products, resulted in a lack of local investment in the most technologically sophisticated components of the branch. Consequently, these links in the productive chain were lost –a phenomenon which was common in all the countries of the region.

In Colombia, the electronic industry survived despite its limited scope by concentrating investment in certain niches in the local market. Of the remaining countries, only Argentina has an electronic industry of any significance. However, transnationals generally prefer to locate their affiliates in Brazil due to the size of the latter's market and the fact that costs are far higher in Argentina.

- *Textiles and clothing:* In the aggregate, the textiles, clothing and leather industries were negatively affected by trade liberalization in almost all countries of the region, to the extent that all such activities were characterized by low investment in the post-reform period. By investing in modernization, however, two countries (Colombia and Peru) were able to achieve a recovery, although not in every subsector. In Peru, investment in the textile industry staged a full recovery between 1994 and 1997 after falling to less than 50% of the historical average. In the case of Colombia, investment in the clothing industry exceeded the average of the pre-reform period by 97%. Investments targeted at both the domestic and foreign markets, together with the quality of raw materials in these countries, allowed the branch to withstand foreign competition. Finally, the growth of the clothing industry in Mexico deserves special mention, having become the principal supplier to the United States market.

- *Mechanical and electrical equipment:* This branch encountered great difficulties with economic liberalization, after having grown significantly in Argentina, Brazil and Mexico towards the end of the import substitution process and then contracting since the 1980s. The reforms highlighted problems of inadequate scale, specialization and technological capacity; a decisive blow was dealt by policies which led appreciation of the local currency.

C. INVESTMENT GROWTH AND SECTORAL PERFORMANCE

Having examined the industrial branches with the highest investment growth, it is worth asking whether strong investment led to greater value added and productivity.

1. Value Added and Productivity

The most dynamic branches with respect to investment also saw their value added and productivity expand more rapidly than the less dynamic branches (see table II-4). Chile registered the strongest gains in value added, after a surge in investment in modernizing the productive apparatus and expanding capacity. Colombia and Mexico followed in terms of production increases.

Table II-4

STRUCTURE OF INVESTMENT, OUTPUT AND PRODUCTIVITY BY LEVEL OF INVESTMENT GROWTH

Country	Investment (Share of total)			Value added (Share of total)			Labour productivity (Index of period average pre-reform = 100)	
	Pre-reform	Post-reform	Consolidated model	Pre-reform	Post-reform	Consolidated model	Post-reform	Consolidated model
Argentina	1991	1996		1970-1989	1992-1996		1992-1996	
More dynamic group	71	79		65	73		195	
Less dynamic group	29	21		35	26		171	
Total	100	100		100	100		191	
Brazil	1980-1989	1995-97		1970-1989	1995-1996		1995-1996	
More dynamic group	44	57		45	50		172	
Less dynamic group	56	43		55	50		161	
Total	100	100		100	100		167	
Colombia	1970-1989	1990-95		1970-1989	1990-1996		1990-1996	
More dynamic group	58	67		60	60		142	
Less dynamic group	42	33		40	40		155	
Total	100	100		100	100		148	
Chile	1960-1973	1986-89	1990-97	1970	1986-1989	1990-1995	1986-1989	1990-1995
More dynamic group		66	80	53	65	65	139	150
Less dynamic group		34	20	47	35	35	133	156
Total		100	100	100	100	100	142	158
Mexico	1970-1985	1991-94		1970-1985	1991-1994		1991-1994	
More dynamic group	44	61		49	53		157	
Less dynamic group	56	39		51	47		146	
Total	100	100		100	100		151	
Peru	1970-1989	1994-95		1970-1989	1994-1996		1994-1996	
More dynamic group	57	73		54	59		80	
Less dynamic group	43	27		46	41		83	
Total	100	100		100	100		82	

Source: Authors' compilation from the database of the research project.

It is interesting to note that even when there was a trend toward increased investment in the most dynamic branches, the overall structure of the branches (that is, the share of each in the total) did not change radically since many of them were already important investment destinations in the pre-reform period. The firms in these branches were thus able to use their experience and the learning process to bolster growth as the reforms were introduced. Nevertheless, the flow of new resources by-passed certain industrial activities which had shown strong growth under the pre-reform model. This was the case for the textiles, footwear and metal tools and equipment sectors.

All the countries significantly improved labour productivity compared to the pre-reform period.[18] Argentina currently has the highest level of labour productivity; it is far above that registered in Colombia, which had a similar evolution of investment. It should be noted that the principal factor explaining the positive trends in productivity has been the extraordinary industrial unemployment throughout the post-reform period.

The varied behaviour of the different branches caused a strong dispersing effect in the value of productivity, even within the group of fast-growing branches. In the case of Chile, for example, some productive branches stagnated while others doubled or even quadrupled the value of productivity in the 25 years following the initiation of the reform process. Executives of firms belonging to the former group are keen to point out that while Chilean firms have indeed acquired cutting-edge technologies for many of their productive processes, other activities maintain a more traditional character. A clear example is the acquisition of latest-technology machinery in production, while activities such as packaging and quality control –which in industrialized countries tend to be automated– continue to be highly labour intensive. These firms face problems of scale and profitability which constrain improvements in labour productivity.

2. Technological Development

Another key question is whether the increase in investment led to technological development. One way of measuring this is by using an indicator which gauges the gap between domestic technology and that found at the global level. Katz (2000) uses regression analysis to estimate the difference in the rate of labour productivity growth in every industrial branch of each country (at the three-digit level of the ISIC) in relation to the corresponding rates in the United States for the periods 1970-1990 and 1970-1996.

The results are presented in table II-5. A number greater than one represents a positive change, while a number below one reflects a widening

---

18   Labour productivity is calculated as the value added in each branch, measured in constant currency, over the number of employees in the branch.

Table II -5
CHANGE IN PRODUCTIVITY GAP IN RELATION TO THE
UNITED STATES, 1970-1996

Investment growth in descending order	Argentina	Brazil	Chile[a/]	Colombia	Mexico[b/]
			1970-1990		
Food products	0.96	0.91	0.72	1.19	1.34
Metal products	1.75	1.08	1.14	1.28	1.40
Other chemical products	1.80	0.7	1.15	1.01	0.79
Chemical industry	1.78	1.12	3.10	1.42	1.16
Plastic products	0.6	0.86	0.73	1.40	1.45
Non-metal minerals	1.19	0.85	1.50	1.69	1.69
Transport equipment	1.01	1.40	1.00	1.44	1.81
Paper and pulp	0.85	1.20	1.61	1.50	1.40
Textiles	1.40	1.48	0.85	1.48	1.01
Clothing	0.80	1.06	0.80	1.01	2.44
Non-electrical machinery	1.47	1.03	1.00	0.79	0.74
Electrical machinery	1.79	1.14	1.00	1.20	1.82
			1970-1996		
Food products	1.10	1.14	0.67	0.93	1.21
Metal products	2.07	1.78	1.22	1.79	1.39
Other chemical products	1.98	0.60	0.97	0.86	0.58
Chemical industry	1.92	1.18	1.79	1.09	0.88
Plastic products	0.81	1.25	0.51	1.50	1.25
Non-metal minerals	2.35	1.28	1.68	1.36	1.39
Transport equipment	2.00	1.33	0.76	2.07	1.81
Paper and pulp	0.99	1.26	1.10	1.12	1.03
Textiles	1.67	1.43	0.77	1.23	0.75
Clothing	1.17	1.20	0.75	1.3	1.85
Non-electrical machinery	1.91	1.12	1.31	0.75	0.72
Electrical machinery	2.68	1.97	0.94	0.99	1.76
			Change 1990-1996		
Food products	+	+	-	-	-
Metal products	+	+	-	+	-
Other chemical products	+	-	-	-	-
Chemical industry	+	+	-	-	-
Plastic products	+	+	-	+	-
Non-metal minerals	+	+	+	-	-
Transport equipment	+	-	-	+	+
Paper and pulp	+	+	-	-	-
Textiles	+	-	-	-	-
Clothing	+	+	-	+	-
Non-electrical machinery	+	+	+	-	-
Electrical machinery	+	+	-	-	-

Source: Authors' compilation based on Jorge Katz, *Reformas estructurales, productividad y conducta tecnológica en América Latina*, Santiago, Chile, Economic Commission for Latin America and the Caribbean (ECLAC)/Fondo de Cultura Económica, 2000.
a/ Through 1995.
b/ Through 1994.

of the gap during the sample period. Comparing the two periods gives an indication of what occurred between 1990 and 1996. In the 1970s and 1980s, for example, productivity in Argentina's food industry displayed a growth rate below that of the United States (the ratio of variation in productivity between the two countries is 0.96). However, the calculation for the 1970-1996 period demonstrates that the gap narrowed (the ratio is 1.10); this is explained by improved performance during the post-reform period.

In the case of Argentina and Brazil, the labour productivity gap in relation to the United States narrowed in the 1990s for all industrial branches, although this was not necessarily related to investment growth. Instead, it is explained by the marked reduction in the workforce and general rationalization undertaken by firms in the years following the introduction of reforms.

Some branches experienced a reverse trend, in which the gap had been narrowing prior to 1990, but widened thereafter. Examples include the "other chemicals" category in both Chile and Colombia and the food and electrical machinery industries in the latter. Mexico is the one country that definitely did not see a noticeable narrowing of the productivity gap in the post-reform period. It is possible, however, that this process may have occurred after 1994 in response to the policy adjustments which followed the Tequila crisis.

The exercise leads to two conclusions. First, there was not an investment drive which led directly to the acquisition of cutting-edge technology. Second, technological progress had historical precedents. As shown in table II-5 with the index for the period 1970-1990, it occurred in the productive branches that were already developing in this regard prior to the introduction of reforms.

3. Market Orientation

One of the objectives of economic liberalization was to reorient industrial products from the domestic to the foreign market. This strategy became widespread in the 1990s, but the degree of success varied across countries.

-    In Chile and Mexico investment growth shows a clear correlation with that of exports. While Chile achieved a high degree of diversification in its export markets thanks to trade with Asian and European countries, the growth of the Mexican export sector was closely tied to the United States market.
-    The reorientation of Chile's production to foreign markets was consolidated between 1986 and 1989, when firms mounted a comprehensive export drive. This phenomenon was extended to industrial branches which historically had no export record, as these benefited from synergies between macroeconomic policies and reform instruments and from the numerous incentives provided by the State. Export growth continued into the 1990s, but it became increasingly concentrated in

activities associated with the processing of natural resources. This encompassed a relatively small number of productive branches characterized by fragile productive linkages and volatile international prices.

- In Mexico, the development of the export sector triggered an investment drive in the automotive, computer, electronic and clothing industries, as firms aimed to improve competitiveness in order to increase market share in the NAFTA area. Investment in export-oriented industries had its first boost in the 1980s and early 1990s; the devaluation which marked the beginning of the Tequila crisis triggered a second boost in the latter half of the 1990s. Clearly, the exchange rate appreciation which took place between 1990 and 1994 delayed the reorientation of production towards foreign markets in certain industrial branches. The export sector comprises affiliates of transnational corporations and medium-sized and large national enterprises with links to transnationals and with access to foreign finance.

- In the case of Argentina, investment growth was associated with both the domestic market and Mercosur. The branches that benefited from this were, in the first instance, those linked directly or indirectly to the special schemes operating in the automotive industry; second, those associated with the processing of natural resources; and finally, those producing other consumption goods with important markets in Mercosur and particularly in Brazil.

- Finally, Brazil, Colombia and Peru retained a growth model based on the domestic market, and they fostered only marginal export growth. In the case of Brazil, the Mercosur market has not made it to the top of the entrepreneurial agenda despite its considerable importance. Due to Brazil's size, it is possible that an inward looking tendency will prevail in the post-reform period, even if the exchange rate recovers from the devaluation of recent years. According to a survey carried out among 730 firms, the emphasis on the domestic market is not inconsistent with an increasing export coefficient in a context of prices favourable to the sector (Bielschowsky 1999a). This confirms that the historical development of the manufacturing industry is similar to that observed in larger, more developed economies, where exports are a consequence of good performance in the domestic market.

- According to Ramírez and Núñez (1999), the investment drive in Colombia was not only the result of the growth in domestic demand, but was also stimulated by the tougher competition in a more open environment and the new dynamics generated by export-oriented industrial activities. Their study does not enable us to draw a causal relation between investment and exports, even after taking into account the general effort to re-direct part of output to foreign markets in

Figure II-1
SHARE OF INDUSTRIAL EXPORTS IN GDP AND TOTAL EXPORTS

ARGENTINA

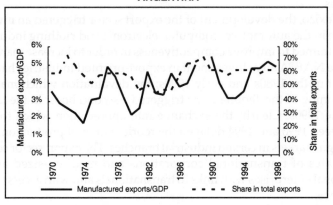

BRAZIL

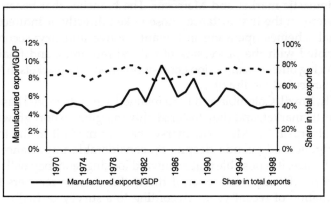

CHILE

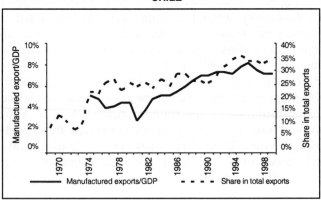

Figure II-1 continued

COLOMBIA

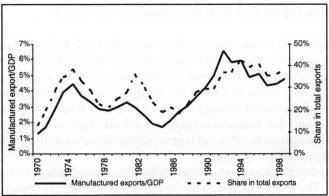

MEXICO

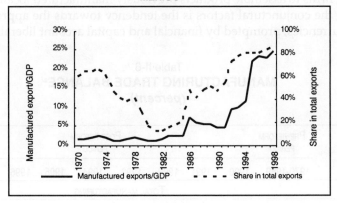

PERU

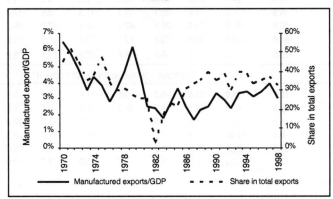

Source: Foreign Trade Data Base for Latin America and the Caribbean (Banco de Datos del Comercio Exterior de América Latina y el Caribe, BADECEL), Economic Commission for Latin America and the Caribbean (ECLAC).

branches which have experienced little change in investment levels. Future export growth in these areas will be limited.

Despite a dynamic export performance, the trade balance of the industrial sector is deteriorating. Indeed, the positive relation between investment and export growth did not prevent a deterioration in the trade balance of the manufacturing sector in five of the sample countries. Table II-6 presents an indicator of the trade balance as a share of the total trade both for the dynamic branches and for manufacturing as a whole. Not only was this balance markedly negative in 1998, but it generally suffered a significant deterioration over the pre-reform average.

This deterioration is explained by both structural factors and conjunctural policies. The former include a tendency within industry to source production inputs from abroad, the breakdown of productive chains and a propensity among firms to assemble products previously manufactured locally. Notable among the conjunctural factors is the tendency towards the appreciation of local currencies, prompted by financial and capital account liberalization.

Table II-6
MANUFACTURING TRADE BALANCE[a]
(percent)

COUNTRY	PRE-REFORM PERIOD	POST-REFORM PERIOD								
	1970-1989	1990	1991	1992	1993	1994	1995	1996	1997	1998
		TOTAL MANUFACTURING								
Argentina	-2.7	44.1	4.5	-27.1	-28.2	-32.2	-14.8	-19.4	-23.7	-27.0
Brazil	12.4	24.1	21.3	30.0	19.2	9.3	-9.3	-9.0	-14.2	-13.6
Chile a/	-6.9	.0	-1.4	-10.1	-19.1	-11.5	-9.6	-17.4	-17.1	-20.6
Colombia	-50.6	-35.9	-20.8	-36.5	-47.3	-49.8	-47.2	-46.2	-50.1	-49.5
Mexico	-44.4	-30.2	-36.8	-23.9	-19.0	-19.1	-1.1	-1.0	-3.1	-5.1
Peru	-10.0	3.6	1.2	-8.2	-16.6	-20.8	-27.1	-23.8	-21.2	-25.6
		SECTORS POSTING INVESTMENT GROWTH								
Argentina	15.1	55.9	28.4	-0.7	-3.8	-11.8	5.7	3.5	-0.3	-2.8
Brazil	38.6	40.3	38.1	45.7	32.0	19.3	-0.8	1.5	-4.4	-4.4
Chile a/	6.5	-8.6	-7.1	-5.5	-13.3	-7.0	-5.6	-12.9	-14.9	-15.5
Colombia	-8.1	14.45	17.2	-1.5	-10.5	-14.7	-17.3	-18.3	-22.1	-16.4
Mexico	-37.3	-25.9	-29.0	-15.0	-9.8	-9.1	6.1	8.3	5.2	3.7
Peru	13.2	20.3	18.2	-1.4	2.8	5.0	-3.7	-3.0	4.8	-19.2

Source: Authors' compilation based on information from Foreign Trade Data Base for Latin America and the Caribbean (Banco de Datos del Comercio Exterior de América Latina y el Caribe, BADECEL), Economic Commission for Latin America and the Caribbean (ECLAC).
a/ Trade balance (X-M)/total trade (X+M).

D. HETEROGENEITY OF COUNTRY PERFORMANCE

Just as sectors and firms demonstrated considerable heterogeneity in performance, marked differences can also be seen in investment behaviour across countries during the transition process.

1. The Determinants of Industrial Investment

Table II-7 presents the main factors determining this behaviour, which in analytical terms can be classified as follows: (a) elements of business strategies, (b) microeconomic strengths and weaknesses and (c) macroeconomic strengths and weaknesses. All of these factors are associated with phenomena which in some cases will be temporary and in others permanent.[19]

The factors motivating business strategy include the re-orientation of production towards foreign markets; the strategic re-positioning on the part of transnational corporations following the introduction of reforms; and the use of new machinery and equipment to raise competitiveness. These elements are all transitory. They were particularly important in those countries where industry entered the second phase of the transition process during the 1990s.

The impact of microeconomic strengths and weaknesses refers mainly to the degree of import penetration and the capacity of firms to defend themselves –a transitory factor which later disappears with industrial restructuring– and to the size of firms dominating the market.

Finally, the factors associated with the macroeconomic context are those elements which have a permanent bearing on investment: variations in demand, macroeconomic stability and variations in the cost of capital, the exchange rate and real interest rates.

2. The Industrial Investment Process by Country

The heterogeneity in industrial investment is a result of differences in macro- and microeconomic contexts and the impact on these of institutional changes. With regard to the investment phases, in the 1990s there was one country (Peru) where industry was dominated by a process of rationalization; three countries (Argentina, Brazil and, from 1994 onwards, Colombia) which

---

19 That is to say, they are recognized in economic theory as determinants of investment in any historical process.

Table II-7
DETERMINANTS OF INVESTOR BEHAVIOUR IN MANUFACTURING IN THE 1990s

Determinant	Chile	Peru	Argentina	Brazil	Mexico	Colombia
BUSINESS STRATEGIES						
Shift to export-oriented output	P	P	P	N	P	N
Strategic repositioning of transnationals	N	N	P	P	M/P	N
Increase in competitiveness (modernization)	M	N/M	P	P	P	P
MICROECONOMIC STRENGTHS AND WEAKNESSES						
Degree of import penetration	M/N	N	N	N	N	N
Average size of firms	M	N	M	M	M	N
MACROECONOMIC ENVIRONMENT						
Growth of industrial demand ("accelerator effect")	P	M	P	N	N	N
Macroeconomic stability (balanced fundamental variables)	P	M	N	N	N	M/N
Real interest rates	P	N/M	M	N	M	M
Variation of real exchange rate	P/M	N	N	N	N	P/M
Variation in capital goods prices	M	P	P	P	M	M

Source: Authors' compilation from the database of the research project.
P= Positive impact on investment
N= Negative impact on investment
M= Moderate impact on investment

initiated a modernization drive; one country (Mexico) where the second phase was characterized by a combined effort to modernize and expand; and lastly, one country (Chile) where industry enjoyed strong investment growth during the consolidation of the new model, which led to increased capacity (table II-8). As mentioned in earlier sections, this does not mean that all industrial branches and firms display this behaviour, but rather that such behaviour predominated within industry at a generalized level.

Table II-8
INDUSTRIAL INVESTMENT BEHAVIOUR IN THE 1990s

COUNTRY	RATIONALIZATION	MODERNIZATION	GROWTH
Argentina	+	+	
Brazil	+	+	
Colombia	+	+	
Chile		+	+
Mexico	+	+	+
Peru	+		

Source: Authors' compilation from the database of the research project.

a. The Industrial Sector in Argentina

To understand the development of the Argentine industrial sector in the 1990s, it is necessary to take into account that one set of reforms had already been introduced in the 1970s. Even though the debt crisis reversed the process, this early liberalization drive –together with the extreme uncertainty and instability generated by the hyperinflation of the late 1980s– speeded up rationalization within firms. The new period of liberalization was undertaken in more favourable macroeconomic conditions, which contributed to further progress in modernization.

In effect, when the stabilization plan was initiated in 1990, a number of projects were salvaged after having been cancelled, postponed, or deemed impossible to develop during the macroeconomic turbulence of the 1980s. Also in contrast to the previous decade, a high proportion of total investment was in machinery, usually of foreign origin. In this way, economic liberalization and the control of exchange rate risk facilitated the process of modernizing machinery and equipment. Even though price stability contributed significantly to the re-activation of investment, however, the uncertainty generated by internal (the fiscal deficit) and external disequilibria did not create an adequate climate for investment in expansion.

As highlighted in a study of the investment behaviour of 1,500 Argentine firms, "the nature of productive capacity incorporation in factories during the 1990s was characterized by the low level of plant construction... and a strong emphasis on technological modernization" (Bisang and Gómez, 1999, p. 48). That is to say, the process of investment in Argentina between 1992 and 1997 was predominantly concentrated in the transition stage of the modernization process, and to a lesser degree in the more advanced stage of expansion. In support of this argument, it is worth noting that during this period the average growth rate for investment in industrial machinery and equipment was 17.3%, compared to 4.9% for investment in construction. This suggests that firms invested relatively little in new plants or in the expansion of existing ones. Nonetheless, some industrial branches and firms pursued a strategy of local and regional growth, for which they adopted an offensive position by expanding their productive capacity while at the same time acquiring advanced technology.

The development among firms and branches was not homogeneous. As indicated by Bisang and Gómez (1999), the shift from macroeconomic uncertainty to microeconomic uncertainty in a context of greater stability led to the design of highly heterogeneous strategies.

Large industrial firms with links to national conglomerates account for a significant percentage of the growth in sectoral investment. For these firms, growth was concentrated in the clothing, oil, electrical machinery, automotive, metal products, plastic products and paper branches.

The business strategy of transnationals was geared toward consolidating market share, improving competitiveness in order to export –particularly to Brazil– and modernizing the capital stock to compete successfully with imports in those sectors oriented to the domestic market. Subsidiaries of transnational corporations concentrated their investments in the following branches: tobacco, electrical machinery manufactures, metal products manufactures, clothing, paper, oil and derivatives, chemical substances, rubber and plastics.

By 1996 capital allocation was re-oriented to the last three branches. These shared certain characteristics: they employed mature technologies, they were based on natural resources, and they had the capacity for large-scale production oriented at the broader Mercosur market. Economies of scale pertained in sectors experiencing investment growth not only among firms associated with the national economic conglomerates, but also among the subsidiaries of transnational corporations.

Furthermore, Bisang and Gómez (1999) show that in the 1990s these groups of firms invested heavily in machinery and equipment, although in contrast to the previous decade the equipment was mostly of foreign origin. New plants were also established in certain branches: food and beverages (dairy products, beer, confectionery, pastas, oils), ceramics, medicines, and iron and steel products.

No capacity expansion occurred in sectors considered key at the global level: electronics, new materials and pharmo-chemicals. Investments of this type were concentrated among a limited number of firms.

Small and medium-sized firms performed well in some sectors, modernizing machinery and equipment of a predominantly domestic origin.

Finally, a large number of industrial branches were adversely affected by liberalization and appreciation of the local currency, to the extent that they were unable to recover during the last decade. The small average size and general weakness of these firms made it very difficult for them to withstand competition.

b. The Industrial Sector in Brazil

The persistent hyperinflation prevailing in the early 1990s was the principal factor prolonging the rationalization process in Brazil, with the modernization stage not getting underway until the mid-1990s.

A survey of investment behaviour carried out among 730 large firms in 1998 shows that priorities in firm strategy included cost-reducing investment, the resolution of problems associated with certain bottlenecks, the replacement of equipment and quality improvements (Bielschowsky, 1999a). A short cycle of modernization followed stabilization. The recorded investment rates did not reach the levels attained in the 1970s, however, but rather were closer to those observed in the 1980s. Bielschowsky (1999a) concludes that a drive to modernize did take place, but this was concentrated in a relatively small group of branches, almost all producing consumer goods.

Between 1995 and 1997 –the period covered by the investment survey– aggregate industrial growth was low, as was export performance. This leads to the conclusion that in contrast to other countries, Brazil did not reorient output to the foreign market. Nor did Brazilian firms prioritize the Mercosur market to the extent that their Argentine counterparts did.

The low stimulus derived from both the meagre growth of the domestic market and general macroeconomic instability was offset in the case of transnational corporations by the need to improve their future position in the Brazilian market. In contrast to the rest of Latin America, progress in economic liberalization allowed the Brazilian market –by virtue of its size– to generate its own momentum, thereby attracting transnationals. Brazil also experienced a lesser degree of microeconomic fragility, due to a relatively lower penetration of imports and the relatively large size of its firms.

The stabilization model, featuring the revaluation of the currency and the introduction of an exchange rate anchor with the consequent unfavourable effect on the profitability of tradable goods, provoked great uncertainty among firms. The growing fiscal and balance-of-payments deficits generated negative expectations of future economic development. As a consequence, the Brazilian stabilization model had to co-exist with domestic interest rates far above those prevailing in the rest of the countries.

Domestic interest rates were virtually prohibitive for investment purposes, with the exception of the interest rates on loans from the State development bank, Banco Nacional de Desarrollo Económico y Social (BNDES), which were around 10% per year in real terms. This explains why firms preferred to concentrate their investment in cost-reducing modernization, financed partly by BNDES and partly with foreign credits. Such investments embodied an extremely high marginal productivity of capital, so high, in fact, that it compensated for the financial cost. While the high cost of capital slowed investment in expansion, this type of investment nevertheless occurred in branches dominated by foreign firms with access to foreign financing.

c.   *The Industrial Sector in Colombia*

After a brief and ephemeral recovery in investment geared towards adjustment and expansion, the increases in industrial investment in Colombia were directed primarily to capital replenishment, the purchase of parts, accessories and office equipment and, in general, the introduction of processes that did not increase existing capacity. They did, however, contribute to more efficient output and administrative processes, as well as to the profitability of firms (Ramírez and Núñez, 1999).

The macroeconomic climate was more stable than that prevailing in the other countries at the time of the reforms, and the country's microeconomic strength was greater in relation to the smaller countries in the study. Consequently, industrial investment did not fall in the first post-reform stage as it did in the other countries. While these conditions were not sufficient to produce investment geared toward expansion of capacity, the benign macroeconomic climate quickly gave rise to "defensive" cost-reducing investment, which partially compensated for the microeconomic fragility and allowed the challenges posed by institutional changes and market liberalization to be met on better terms.

The investment surveys carried out periodically in Colombia show that investment was concentrated in the modernization of equipment designed to substitute obsolete capital and increase the competitiveness of national industry. This led to important improvements in productivity. Disincentives for investment in expansion came from the relatively marginal growth in demand, the low income elasticity of supply (which was indicative of the lack of competitiveness of domestic industry) and the instability of the principal markets for Colombian industrial exports (Venezuela and the rest of the Andean Pact).

Judging by the increase in import penetration, which was inferior only to that registered in Mexico, liberalization introduced a high degree of uncertainty into investment decisions. Another factor contributing to increased uncertainty was the smaller size of industrial firms relative to those in Brazil, Argentina, and Mexico.

d.   *The Industrial Sector in Chile*

Over the course of the last 25 years, four stages can be identified in the development of investment in the Chilean industrial sector. Two of these took place during the transition process, while the remaining two appeared during the process of consolidating the new economic model created by the reforms

(Moguillansky, 1999). The four stages are as follows: (a) the reallocation of capital assets and low investment, brought about by the drastic changes generated by the economic transformations and by macroeconomic signals inconsistent with an investment effort; (b) the modernization of production in the processing of natural resources and in activities exposed to competition in foreign markets, in which the State played a fundamental role in supporting and strengthening the private sector; (c) productive consolidation and expansion, characterized by dynamic investment during the first half of the 1990s, which coincided with the model's consolidation phase; and (d) the restructuring of conglomerates and the deepening of globalization in the later 1990s, characterized by a trend toward slower investment growth in the export sectors which had underpinned the growth model.

The economic groups have been key to this development. They took advantage of the direct stimulus provided by the second stage of privatizations –from 1986 onwards– to rearticulate conglomerates, redirect resources towards activities enjoying natural comparative advantages, increase competitiveness and capture new foreign markets.

This strategy demanded new and significant investment, which enjoyed State support throughout the period covering the second stage of the investment process: there was a correction in relative prices (including a sustained decline in interest rates, a devaluation of the local currency and slow growth in wages), resource transfers, debt-for-equity swaps –which implied strong subsidies for capital entering the economy as foreign investment– and numerous export promotion policies.

Certain factors nevertheless hindered the sustained growth of industrial investment, such as the high concentration of investment in a few branches and activities. An analysis of these branches suggests that the business cycle peaked by the beginning of 2000. This phenomenon may have several explanations, including the decreasing return to capital in some activities, the reduction of incentives provided by the State, reductions in world prices (which affected many branches that had become leading exporters of certain products), the appreciation of the local currency, the emergence of new actors, increasing competition, declining profitability and the introduction of stricter and more comprehensive market regulation (clearly visible in the Chilean financial market, stock exchange, and environmental requirements, among others). Firms reacted to these changes by searching abroad for profits similar to those generated at the start of the privatization process. This development corresponds to a structural shift, which was exacerbated by the effects of the Asian crisis.

e.   *The Industrial Sector in Mexico*

Although Mexican industry embarked on a process of rationalization as soon as the recovery from the 1982 crisis got underway, this process was prolonged by the growing pressures from the liberalization that was initiated in the middle of the decade. The period was characterized by low levels of fixed investment, although a recovery did begin in 1991.

From the mid-1980s onwards, the change in the strategy of large Mexican firms was driven by growing integration with the United States, which was sealed in 1994 with the NAFTA treaty. In the 1990s, and with transnational corporations at the helm, the industrial branches that had been at the forefront of growing integration with the United States (namely, the automotive, electronic and assembly plant operations) became the fastest growing branches, rapidly expanding productive capacity (Calderón, Mortimore and Peres, 1995). However, these were an exception to a mediocre aggregate performance of investment.

By 1994, considerable progress in price stability had not been sufficient to generate confidence with respect to future macroeconomic performance. Exchange rate appreciation, trade deficits and, from 1992 onwards, the rise in domestic interest rates led to a cautious attitude among firms producing for the domestic market.

This context increased the degree of heterogeneity within industry. The stagnant, least competitive branches –dominated by small and medium-sized firms (footwear, clothing, mechanical equipment)– benefited very little from the recovery of the domestic market owing to their lack of competitiveness. In contrast, the dynamic branches were able to strengthen and adjust to the challenges of foreign trade, combining increases in domestic sales with export growth, even in a context of exchange rate appreciation.

The evaluation of the Mexican industrial sector by Moreno-Brid (1999), based on data for the mid-1990s, is not positive. The upgrading of the productive apparatus was incomplete or insufficient to meet the levels of competition prevailing in global markets. Mattar and Peres (1999) confirm this assertion: both transnationals and large national firms, many of which are exporters, headed the process of capital formation, while the rest of the industrial sector (made up of small and medium-sized firms) found itself marginalized from the modernization process due to the scarcity of investment funds.

Perhaps unlike any other country, Mexico suffered for having combined trade liberalization with an appreciating currency. This is confirmed by the fact that import penetration in Mexico was well above that observed in any of the other countries studied. Integrating with the United States market was a radical policy choice for Mexico, and one that was heavily dependent on the exchange rate. However, exchange rate policy was geared more toward price stabilization than toward improving the relative competitiveness of the productive sectors.

Consequently, a negative synergy developed between the microeconomic uncertainty generated by liberalization and the macroeconomic uncertainty derived from the stabilization model. This notwithstanding, an export boom developed following the Tequila crisis, with the virtuous combination of exchange rate depreciation and the fruits of steady investment in export-oriented sectors. This may foster growth in industrial investment, although data are not available to corroborate this view.

Business strategies have been partly geared towards assembly activities (maquila). According to Mendiola (1999), the assembly plant industry was the only sector that grew steadily after the early 1980s. This pattern became even more marked during the 1990s. By 1997, the maquila sector comprised 2,717 firms producing a high proportion of Mexico's total exports (US$ 45 billion, primarily in automotive parts, electric and electronic products and textiles and clothing). Annual investment in the maquila sector between 1993 and 1997 reached US$ 2.4 billion, with a strong upward trend (rising from US$ 1.1 billion in 1993 to US$ 3.1 billion in 1997). To provide a better idea of magnitude, we have calculated that annual investment in all non-assembly manufacturing averaged US$ 5.3 billion between 1991 and 1994, or just over double the average annual investment in the assembly industry in the 1993-1997 period.

f. The Industrial Sector in Peru

Peruvian industry was weakened by the economic and political instability of the 1980s. The capacity of industrial enterprises to adopt defensive strategies in the face of liberalization was adversely affected not only by hyperinflation, but also by stabilization measures. Economic reform therefore contributed more to the weakening of the sector than to its strengthening. In contrast to the other countries, it is not possible to observe any significant subsector enjoying a more positive trend.

The low levels of industrial investment are explained by the high incidence of idle capacity, severe microeconomic weaknesses, the absence of any stimulus from export-oriented production, and a lack of interest on the part of transnationals in achieving positions in the domestic market. Aside from the foodstuffs branch, transnationals have not been incorporated into Peruvian industry. This explains as well the low levels of investment in modernization and cost-reduction. As a result, Peruvian industry was still in the rationalization stage at the end of the 1990s.

Such microeconomic uncertainty combined with and was fuelled by the relatively unfavourable macroeconomic conditions that hindered investment decisions. The stabilization of prices and of political and social conditions introduced the bare minimum in terms of the necessary conditions for a recovery in investment, as did the new equilibrium in public finances. However, industrial investment was hindered by high interest rates and a potentially destabilizing current account deficit. This external disequilibrium generated uncertainty about future macroeconomic performance, and it introduced a considerable degree of caution into investment decisions.

CHAPTER III

INVESTMENT IN THE MINING AND HYDROCARBON SECTORS

■

The mining and hydrocarbon sectors have certain characteristics in common.[20] Not only do they stem from the same source, but the two sectors account for a considerable proportion of fiscal revenue and total exports in many countries in the region. The importance of oil and gas in energy generation also means that they are significant components of the countries' infrastructure. Historically, these productive activities have undergone periods of domination by transnational capital and periods of complete State control.

Toward the end of the 1990s, institutional change accelerated to the extent that some countries actually privatized their State-owned mineral and hydrocarbon deposits outright. However, the economic power of these firms and the strategic nature of the product –particularly in the case of oil, which is crucial to the global competitiveness of an economy– forced most countries to approach the privatization process with caution. They thus formed strategic partnerships with transnational capital instead of privatizing, and they passed legislation to regulate the monopolistic markets, fix tariffs and ensure security of supply.

Consequently, a variety of different situations arose in the region's mining and hydrocarbon sectors in the 1990s. In some countries firms were sold off entirely, while in others the State retained a strong presence. In all countries, however, a process of internationalization took place which was linked not

---

20 The information contained in the text, tables, boxes and figures in this chapter comes from the database of the research project. It is taken from the following authors and bibliographical references: Campodónico (1999b, 1999c); Moguillansky (1998b); de Moori Koening (1999); Soares (1998); Ayala (1998); Fainboim and Rodriguez (2000); Gadano (1998); Oliveira (1999); Torres (1999).

only to foreign trade, but also to the participation of transnational companies in sectoral investment.

Because the development of the mining sector and the extraction of hydrocarbons depend primarily on the availability of the resources, this study focuses on those countries which have large mineral deposits. In the case of mineral products, we concentrate on four of the eight countries: Argentina, Brazil, Chile and Peru. In the case of hydrocarbons, we examine Argentina, Bolivia, Brazil, Colombia, Mexico and Peru.

A particular characteristic of these sectors is that a large amount of capital is required before exploitation projects can be developed to full capacity. This means that the period between discovering deposits and exploiting them depends in large part on the prevailing characteristics and situation of the markets in which the minerals and hydrocarbons will be sold. Consequently, the market determines the timing of investment, and even when specific investment incentives are in place, the investment response can take several years. Institutional changes must be accompanied by positive signals in the international market in order to attract investment.

A. THE INTERNATIONAL MINERAL AND HYDROCARBON MARKETS

Since these resources are mostly sold on the international market, investment is largely determined by international prices and medium-term expectations of world demand. In the case of hydrocarbons, the development of the international market can have either a primary or secondary role, depending on the product and specific market segment, that is, the exploration, production, distribution and commercialization of oil, gas and their derivatives.

1. The Evolution of the International Minerals Market

The 1990s was a positive period for Latin American mineral products because of the upturn in world consumption compared with the 1980s and the relative improvement in prices despite the long-term downward trend. At the same time, the availability of financing, in the form of international loans and resources from foreign investors, helped to bring about investment in exploiting the deposits that had been studied and evaluated in the previous decade.

As Sánchez Albavera and others (1998) show, the world market for mineral products is heavily correlated with output and demand growth. Copper, for example, experienced similar levels of growth in production and consumption over the last three decades: in the 1970s, growth rates were 2.03% in production and 2.57% in consumption; in the 1980s, they were 1.55% and 1.41%; and between 1990 and 1997 they were 2.15% and 2.34%, respectively. Expected consumption growth is what stimulates production.

The mining industry experiences periods of expansion and recession as a function of the level of output growth in industrialized countries and in a number of developing countries. Unlike the industrialized countries, this group of developing countries increased their minerals consumption during the 1990s, until the Asian crisis. As a result, world mineral and metals consumption rose from US$ 93 billion to US$ 162 billion between 1980 and 1996. During that period, the participation of developed countries as a whole in total consumption fell from 79% to 65%, while the fastest growing developing countries came to account for 24% of total consumption, up from 10%.[21] Table III-1 shows that consumption of copper, lead and zinc rose sharply between 1990 and 1996 compared with the 1980s, while that of aluminium and tin experienced the continuation of a downward trend.

When consumption is rising and price forecasts show favourable margins over costs, mining activity expands and investors increase the exploitation of deposits. A boom is characterized by rising prices and shrinking stocks. If the cycle also coincides with high levels of liquidity in international markets – demonstrated by a large supply of loans and resources– then large investment projects begin and capital formation accelerates. This occurred between the end of the 1980s and the 1990s, generating a rise in investment in the sector. In contrast, the 1980s were largely characterized by extremely negative prices and demand.

Although consumption growth stimulated supply in the 1990s, real prices of metals experienced a decline (figure III-1), which was exacerbated from 1998 onwards by the Asian and international financial crises. Historically, a fall in prices often led to technological innovation –developed by transnational mining companies– in order to reduce costs and increase the productivity and profitability of deposits. Changes were introduced in all areas of the industry, including the use of computers and satellites in mineral prospecting, new forms of mechanization and automation of operations, the application of new methods for processing minerals, the introduction of automatic control and the use of robots in some operations. Such innovations were particularly prevalent in the exploitation and production of refined iron, copper and gold in the 1980s. They were adopted throughout the Latin American region thanks to foreign investment in mining.

---

21 Figures are taken from United Nations, *Monthly Bulletin of Statistics*, various issues.

Table III-1
GROWTH OF WORLD METAL CONSUMPTION
(annual average growth rates)

METAL	1960-1970	1970-1980	1980-1990	1990-1996
Aluminum	9.0	4.4	2.3	1.3
Copper	4.3	2.6	1.4	2.4
Tin	0.9	0.2	0.6	0.3
Nickel	6.1	2.2	1.6	1.6
Lead	4.1	3.1	0.0	1.3
Zinc	4.8	2.2	0.7	2.4

Source: Metallgesellschaft Aktiengesellschaft, *Metal Statistics,* and World Office of Metal Statistics.

Figure III-1
REAL PRICES OF FIVE METALS, 1980-1999
(Index, 1980 = 100)

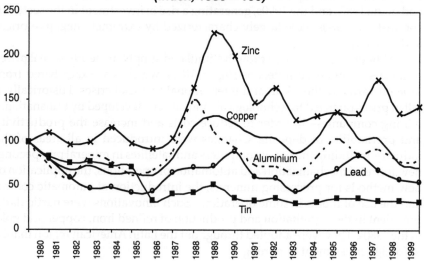

Source: Authors' compilation from the database of the Natural Resources Division, Economic Commission for Latin America and the Caribbean (ECLAC).

2. *The Evolution of the International Hydrocarbon Market*

World GDP growth projections provide the basis for assessing the future evolution of primary energy demand. Population growth, industrialization, urbanization and projections on the availability of non-commercial energy sources also play a role. The latest projections estimate that world demand will grow at an annual average rate of between 2.7% and 3.7% through 2010. International Energy Outlook projects that oil demand in Latin America will double between 1995 and 2020, growing at an annual rate of 4.3%, which is much higher than the forecast for developed countries (1.1%) and very close to the rate projected for Southeast Asia. Demand for natural gas will be even higher: most will be destined for energy generation in developed countries, but demand will also rise in developing countries. In Latin America, it is estimated that this demand will grow by 7% per year over the next twenty years. These projections represent an incentive for new investment in the region, but they should be considered against the backdrop of falling real prices, as Campodónico (1999c) shows. If the trend of recent decades continues, falling profit margins will force oil companies to reduce costs by pursuing technological progress in the exploration and development processes, improving management and business practices and increasing productivity.

Investment in natural gas is likely to increase, since –with the exception of Argentina and Venezuela– the industry in Latin America is still very underdeveloped with respect to production and existing reserves. Increased government efforts in the area of cleaner energy would also foster investment, as it would encourage thermoelectric plants and public transportation to switch from oil and coal inputs to natural gas.

B. INSTITUTIONAL REFORM

In the 1970s, mineral and oil deposits were largely State owned under a policy of defending strategically important natural resources. By the late 1980s and early 1990s, however, the lack of public resources for investing in the exploration, development and exploitation of new deposits generated an opposite trend. Incentives for foreign investment in mining were introduced as part of the structural changes underway in the region. Some of the incentives were provided by the institutional framework, which can be summarized as follows: (a) the treatment of foreign investment in general, (b) changes in oil legislation and in the administrative regime governing mining concessions, (c) changes in the tax regime for mining and hydrocarbons and (d) the privatization of mineral deposits or segments of the hydrocarbon production and distribution chain.

1. Reform of Foreign Investment Laws

Most countries in the region eliminated the barriers to foreign capital, which had been imposed at the national or subregional level during the 1970s. Chile pioneered this reform with the incorporation of Decree Law 600 in 1974. In the early 1990s, other countries used that legislation as a model for liberalizing the conditions of entry, capitalization, and profit remittances, ensuring the stability of taxation and tariffs, and removing discriminatory rules that favoured national investors. Argentina, Brazil and Chile now have laws embodied in the constitution which grant the same treatment to both foreign and national capital, while other countries achieve this with specific legislation[22] (see Table III-2).

Table III-2
CHANGES IN FOREIGN INVESTMENT LAWS

Country	Year	Changes in laws
Argentina	1993	Foreign investment law, Decree 1,853
Bolivia	1990	Investment law No. 1,182
	1991	Decision 291
Brazil	1995	Constitutional amendment
Colombia	1991	International investment statute, based on article No. 100 of the constitution, and article No. 15 of law No. 9
Chile	1974	Foreign investment statute, or decree law 600
Mexico	1993	Foreign investment law
Peru	1992	Foreign investment development law, or legislative decree 662

Source: Authors' compilation from country legislation.

---

22 For a complete review of foreign investment laws, see Moussa (1998) and Sánchez Albavera and others (1998).

2. Changes in Sectoral Legislation

In the 1990s legislation on concessions and contracts for mining and hydrocarbons was modified to reduce the risk and uncertainty for foreign investors. Rules were introduced to maximize the guarantees and legal stability for foreign investment and reduce discretionary authority.

a. Reforms of the Legislation on Mining Concessions

Sánchez Albavera and others (1998) show that economic reforms introduced three types of regimes governing mining concessions. Most countries in the region employ an administrative regime under which the State grants mineral rights through a public administration entity, which takes the place of a mining authority. Chile uses a judicial regime, which differs from normal concessions in that the judiciary holds the power to establish, maintain and revoke concessions without the intervention of another authority. Finally, Venezuela applies a contractual regime, in which the rights and obligations of the concessionaire are formalized by an administrative contract. Colombia is considering similar legislation.

Most regional legislation grants mineral rights for exploration and exploitation; some countries also provide for processing and a few for commercialization. Legislation outlining procedures for obtaining concessions was designed to avoid subjecting the process to regulation in order to promote legal stability and provide greater guarantees for investors. Countries generally tried to reduce discretionary authority to a minimum: in Chile this was achieved through the judicial regime for concessions, while in Peru it came about through "administrative silence" and the "presumption of truth". Legislation establishes that mining claims must be recorded in a special registry maintained by the authorities. Disputes are resolved by the mining court, which is one of the functions of the central mining authority. In the case of Chile, the judiciary exercises jurisdiction. In countries where a concession is protected by the payment of a right or patent, the concession expires if payment is not made (see Table III-3).

Table III-3
PRINCIPAL CHARACTERISTICS OF REFORMS TO
MINING LEGISLATION

COUNTRY	LEGAL REFORMS	CONCESSION REGIME	CHARACTERISTICS OF THE REFORM
Argentina	Legislative changes in 1993 and 1995	Administrative regime	End to exclusive State control of exploitation Elimination of areas reserved for the public company Application of uniform mining policy between the provinces and the executive power; harmonization of procedures in different jurisdictions
Brazil	Constitutional amendment of 1995	Administrative Autional regime	Restoration of equal access to mining for foreign and domestic firms
Chile	Constitution of 1980 Constitutional organic law of 1983	Judicial regime	Establishment of judicial concession regime and judicial term for full concession Definition of concession as an unlimited right; expropriation would require full compensation of commercial value of the concession
Peru	Decree law 708 1992 Article 7 of the land law	Administrative regime	Change to ordinary mining procedures for obtaining a concession Elimination of red tape Creation of a legal framework to solve the problem of access

Source: Authors' compilation from the database of the research project, and Nicole Moussa, "Los cambios en la legislación sobre inversión extranjera directa en ocho países de América Latina", Santiago, Chile, Environment and Development Division, Economic Commission for Latin America and the Caribbean (ECLAC), unpublished.

b. *Reforms of Hydrocarbon Contracts*

In the early 1990s most hydrocarbon-producing countries in the region changed their oil contracting regimes.[23] The changes facilitated a greater participation of foreign capital in oil production, longer time frames for exploration and the so-called seismic option, which eliminated the obligation

---

23   For an in-depth study of Latin American contracting regimes, see Campodónico (1996a).

to drill exploratory wells, thereby helping to reduce the cost of exploration considerably.

Of all the contractual changes, the most radical was that promoted by Argentina in 1989 and implemented between 1990 and 1991, granting exploration and exploitation permits in which the oil or natural gas becomes the property of the concessionaire. Peru followed suit in August 1993, when it passed the new hydrocarbon law, Law 26,221. This law modified the oil contracting rules for exploration and production, granting ownership of the oil and gas to the contractors.

The Bolivian capitalization law converted State firms into mixed corporations. Later, Law 1,689 on hydrocarbons introduced joint-risk contracts with Yacimientos Petroliferos Fiscales Bolivianos (YPFB) for the exploration, exploitation and commercialization of hydrocarbons.

The other countries in the study did not transfer ownership of the firms to the private sector, but legal reforms permitted the participation of private actors in some segments of hydrocarbon production and distribution (see table III-4).

In an effort to stimulate foreign investment, taxes and royalties were also been reduced. Most of the countries in the region introduced changes to the tax laws and specific mining and hydrocarbon laws. Together with the extension of the value added tax (VAT) and the elimination of VAT exemptions, income tax were generally reduced.[24] Guarantees of tax stability were also granted for both mining and hydrocarbons. Both sectors are subject to the same tariff regime.

C. THE NEW MARKET STRUCTURE AND REGULATION

New legislation on foreign investment and on sectoral contracts and concessions encouraged the entry of domestic and foreign private actors into the market. In the mining sector, capital has been introduced largely by transnational corporations that explore for and exploit copper and gold mines, while in the hydrocarbon sector both domestic and foreign firms are active in extraction, production and the distribution of oil and gas. The participation of new actors changed the structure of the markets. Whereas a vertically integrated State monopoly once dominated, a group of firms is now operating in the sector, which introduced considerable competition in some segments.

---

24   See Sánchez Albavera and others (1998) and Montalbán (1997).

1. The Structure of the Mining Sector Market

In the mining sector, State firms were privatized and transnational corporations fought to gain control over new deposits. The new laws did not impose barriers to the participation of new firms, such that any entity can now explore for and exploit reserves. These activities are not regulated, and the price is determined in the international market.

Essentially two types of change occurred in this sector. Some countries (such as Chile from 1974 to present and Brazil until 1996) incorporated private

Table III-4
REFORMS IN HYDROCARBON CONTRACTS

COUNTRY	LEGAL CHANGES	INCORPORATION OF PRIVATE FIRMS	CHANGES IN CONTRACTS
Argentina	Decrees 1989	Transfer of areas for exploration and production to private firms	Exploration and concession permits with royalty payments and oil ownership rights
	1990	Bidding for secondary areas	
	1991	Bidding for central areas	
	1992	Privatization of Gas del Estado	
	1993	Privatization of YPF[a]	
Brazil	1995: Constitutional Amendment No.9	Concessions for private firms in new areas of exploration and production	End to Petrobras[b] monopoly in exploration, production, distribution and refining of hydrocarbons
Bolivia	1996: Law 1,689 on hydrocarbons	Partnership with State company	Shared-risk contracts
Colombia	1994	Change to partnership contract with Ecopetrol[c]	Introduction of the R factor (relation between revenue and expenditure) in distribution of production and reimbursement of productive wells
Peru	1993: Law 26,221 on hydrocarbons	Incorporation of licensing contract	Transfer of property rights over the product; royalty payment to the State

Source: Authors' compilation from the database of the research project.
a/ Yacimientos Petrolíferos Fiscales.
b/ Petróleo Brasileño.
c/ Empresa Colombiana de Petróleos.

actors into the exploration and exploitation of new mineral deposits – transnational firms in large projects and domestic firms in small and medium-sized projects– while the State retained ownership of the State firm. The second approach was to completely sell-off of the publicly owned firm, as occurred in Argentina and Peru starting in 1992 and in Brazil in 1997. The Argentine case is somewhat different, however, in that mining was not an important activity until the 1990s.

Competition in the sector is demonstrated by the active participation of Australian, Canadian, American, English and South African firms in the search for and exploration of new deposits (table III-5). In Chile this process began after the recovery of the international copper market in the mid-1980s, almost five years after the constitutional reform gave foreign investors full protection. It coincided with the recovery of the copper price and greater liquidity in international financial markets. In contrast, the privatization of mineral deposits fostered the entry of foreign capital to Peru.

In Argentina, an infant mining industry was established in the 1990s. This development was fostered not only by structural and regulatory change, but also by the corporate strategies of transnational mining companies, new technology –which allowed the profitable exploitation of deposits that previously could not be mined economically– and the advantages associated with location (including Argentina's considerable, largely unexploited geological potential, the low environmental costs, the mining integration treaty with Chile and the availability of low-cost electricity and natural gas).

2. Market Structure in the Hydrocarbons Sector

With the exception of Mexico, the increased involvement of private actors in the hydrocarbons sector led to the elimination of the State monopoly, in both upstream and downstream activities.[25]

In the case of oil, of the six countries studied, Argentina, Bolivia and Peru privatized the State monopoly as a first step toward decentralizing the firm both vertically and horizontally, incorporating national and transnational firms in exploration, production, commercialization and distribution of oil and derivatives. Brazil opened its market to the private sector in 1995, but only held the first auction for concessions in 1999. In Bolivia, risk capital was incorporated through partnerships with the State firm (see table III-6).

In the case of gas, the 1990s represented the start of a significant growth period in Latin America, as in the rest of the world. As Campodónico (1996b)

---

25 "Upstream" activities in the oil and gas industry are those related to exploration and production of deposits. "Downstream" refers to refining, derivatives production, commercialization and distribution of these products.

Table III-5
PROJECTS INVOLVING TRANSNATIONAL MINING COMPANIES

PROJECT	OWNERS	METAL	COUNTRY OF ORIGIN
ARGENTINA (1990s)			
Minera Andes S.A.	Newcrest Resources, Cominco, Pegasus Gold International	Gold, copper and silver	United States, Canada
Minera Triton	Branch of Triton Mining Corp., Northern Orion Exploration	Gold, silver, copper	Canada
Viceroy Resource Corporation	Bell Coast Corp.	Gold	United States
El Abra S.A.	Apertura Bi-Regional Andina S.A., Cidef Argentina S.A., Cominco Ingeniería y Proyectos	Copper	Canada Argentina
Compañía Minera Antofalla S.A.	Northern Orion Exploration	Copper, lead, silver, zinc and gold	Canada
Bajo La Alumbrera project	Mim Holdings Limited, North Limited, Río Algom Limited	Gold and copper	Australia Canada
CHILE (SINCE THE 1980s)			
Cerro Colorado	Río Algom Ltda.	Copper	Canada
Quebrada Blanca	Cominco, Q.B Resources Ltda.	Copper	Canada
Collahuasi	Falconbridge, Shell, Chevron	Copper	United States
Lince	Outokumpu	Copper	Finland
Iván y Zar	Minera Rayrock Ltda.	Copper	
Zaldívar	Outokumpu	Copper	Finland
Escondida	BHP-Utah, RTZ, Jeco, IFC	Copper	Australia England, Japan
Las Luces	Billiton	Copper	Holland

Table III-5 continued

Project	Owners	Metal	Country of origin
	Chile (since the 1980s)		
La Candelaria	Phelps Dodge	Copper	United States
Pelambres	Anaconda Chile Inc.	Copper	Chile, Japan
Los Bronces	Exxon Minerals Inc.	Copper	United States
El Indio/Tambo	American Barrick	Gold	United States
La Coipa	Placer Dome	Gold	United States
San Cristóbal	Niugini	Gold	Japan
Andacollo	Dayton Developments	Gold	
Guanaco	Amax Gold	Gold	United States
	Peru (1990s)		
Southern Peru Copper Corporation	Asarco, Marmon Group, Phelps Dodge	Copper	United States
Cerro Verde	Cyprus Amax, Buenaventura	Copper	United States Peru
Yanacocha	Newmont, Buenaventura	Gold	United States Peru
Antamina	Noranda, Algom, Río Teck	Copper	Canada

Source: Authors' compilation from the database of the research project.

Table III-6
REFORMS IN THE OIL INDUSTRY

START OF THE PROCESS	PRIVATIZATION MECHANISMS	MARKET STRUCTURE	PRICE REGULATION/DEREGULATION
ARGENTINA			
September 1992, Law 24,135: transferred control of hydrocarbons to provinces Law 21,145: declared total privatization of YPF	Decree 2,778 Transformation of YPF into a corporation; initiation of privatization process in two stages Transformation stage: sale of shares considered unnecessary for future business (January 1991 to December 1992) Restructuring stage: ended in June 1993 with the public sale of 45% of YPF shares	Share of production in 1996: YPF: 46% Perez Companc: 11.9% Petróleos San Jorge: 7.4% Amoco: 6.9% Austral:5.8% Astra: 4.7% Tecpetrol: 3.2% Bridas: 3.0% Pluspetrol: 2.3% Limited competition in commercialization and distribution	Since January 1991: Deregulation of crude oil prices and derivatives prices
BOLIVIA			
1996: Law 1,689 on hydrocarbons	Capitalization process of State firm YPFB Split of YPFB into two companies: Chaco and Andina Incorporation of new private firms in production	Share of production in 1997: Chaco: 35% Andina: 38% Other private: 27% (Diamond Shamrock, Tesoro, Perez Companc, Maxus, Pluspetrol)	Willingness to deregulate prices but until 1998 the government negotiated with producers to establish a price band based on international prices

Table III-6 continued

BRAZIL		
Constitutional amendment 1995 1997: Law 9,478	Opening of exploration, production and distribution to private firms Promotion of open competition in the sector	Share of production in 1997: Petrobras: 100% Partnerships of private investors with the State firm, under negotiation	Prices regulated by the public sector

COLOMBIA		
1994: Modification of partnership contracts with private capital	Did not privatize State firm Partnership with domestic and foreign capital in exploration and exploitation	State monopoly in exploration and production Limited competition in distribution and commercialization	Prices regulated by the public sector

PERU		
Legislative decree 655, 1991: Eliminated State monopoly in exploration, exploitation, commercialization and distribution Privatization: 1992-1993 and 1996-1997	Privatization of Petroperú Sale of shares in the firm Licensing contracts for production shares Sale of shares in the refinery	Sale of production shares Limited competition in distribution and commercialization	Free market rates

Source: Authors' compilation of statistics from the research database.

indicates, this growth was fostered by the discovery of new reserves and the reorientation of energy policy in almost all countries, which began to place a higher priority on environmental concerns. Argentina, Colombia and even Mexico introduced legislative reform and new regulatory frameworks that encouraged the participation of private actors in production (only in Argentina) and in transport and distribution (in all three countries).

This led to significant development of the Argentine gas industry, which traditionally was hindered by regulations and low prices. The discovery of the Cuenca Austral and Noroeste reserves, in addition to the mega-deposits at Loma de Lata in Neuquén, have forced private producers to find new applications, thereby increasing the vertical integration of the value chain with petrochemicals, on the one hand, and electricity generation, on the other, providing the inputs for combined cycle plants. Large reserves have recently been discovered in Colombia, where the regulatory framework and incorporation of private capital in the gas pipeline network facilitated a sharp increase in the domestic and industrial use of natural gas. In Mexico, this process has just started.

The new structure adopted by different market segments generated new rules for setting prices. In the countries in which hydrocarbon production is still in State hands, prices are fixed by a governmental authority. In Argentina and Peru, which established a competitive market, prices are unregulated. Prices of oil derivatives are generally set by the market, with the international price strongly influencing the domestic price.

With the exception of Argentina, gas prices are regulated, with tariffs set as a function of production, transport and distribution costs. The consumer price is the sum of these three components, to which are added national and provincial taxes in some countries. The costs cover investment and a reasonable profit margin, which is negotiated between the authorities and companies (see table III-7).

D. FIRM STRATEGIES AND TYPES OF FINANCING

Sectoral reforms and incentives to encourage new entrants into the mining and hydrocarbon sectors led to new business development strategies. These were implemented not only by transnational corporations but also by public firms, boosting the growth of the sector, in particular capital accumulation. The new strategies were compatible with the process of globalization and internationalization of productive markets and financing.

Table III-7
REFORMS IN THE GAS INDUSTRY

START OF THE PROCESS	PRIVATIZATION MECHANISMS	MARKET STRUCTURE	PRICE REGULATION/DEREGULATION
ARGENTINA			
Law 24.076 1992: approve privatization of Gas del Estado Define sectoral regulatory framework	Transfer areas of production to private firms Sale of gas pipelines to two firms in different geographical locations Definition of eight geographical areas for distribution	Output market: open competition Transport: geographical monopolies Distribution market: eight firms in each of the geographical areas	Free market rate for output Regulated transport and distribution prices: reflect cost plus a "reasonable" profit Consumer price: sum of producer price plus transport tariff, plus national and provincial taxes
COLOMBIA			
Law 142 1994: law of public domestic services	Participation in partnership with Ecopetrol, in exploration and production Concessions, or type of build, operate and transfer to State Sale of shares in distribution	State monopoly in exploration and production Transport concessions Limited competition in distribution and commercialization	Prices regulated by public sector Producer prices: changing calculation Transport prices: consider loads of connection and loads of use, and set maximum tariff for three years Consumer prices: sum of production price, plus transport tariff, plus distribution tariff, plus national and provincial taxes
MEXICO			
1995: modification of regulatory law of article 27 of the constitution March 1996: creation of Energy regulatory commission	Incorporation of private or foreign firms in transport, storage, distribution and commercialization	Developing process of granting permits Building new pipelines	Prices regulated by Energy Regulatory Commission

Source: Authors' compilation from the database of the research project.

1. Firm Strategies

Since the international market is the primary destination of the products from these sectors, State firms as well as subsidiaries of transnational corporations have had to work hard to modernize their productive processes and machinery and equipment to reduce costs and compete globally.

In the hydrocarbon sector, the State continues to be the main player in the Latin American market, through firms such as Petróleos de Venezuela, S.A. (PDVSA) in Venezuela; Petróleo Brasileiro (PETROBRAS) in Brazil; Petróleos Mexicanos (PEMEX) in Mexico; PETROECUADOR, the Ecuadoran State oil company; and the Empresa Colombiana de Petróleos (ECOPETROL) in Colombia. In mining, Chile has the only important State-owned company, namely, the Corporación Nacional del Cobre de Chile (CODELCO-Chile), since the Brazilian Compañía Vale do Río Doce (CVRD) was privatized in 1997.

The modernization of management led to the introduction of decentralized administrative bodies grouped by business area, each of which is an independent profit centre, and to the incorporation of a holding company that controls the various business units of the firm. This process occurred in PDVSA, PEMEX, PETROBRAS, and ECOPETROL. In the case of CODELCO-Chile, organizational change is a legislative matter for the national congress, but since recent governments have not made CODELCO a priority, the firm has opted to strengthen corporate development without legally separating its various divisions.

To foster growth and increase world market share, these state firms introduced a number of policies that vary considerably from earlier strategies. In particular, the firms sought strategic partnerships with transnational corporations for exploration and exploitation contracts for mineral and hydrocarbon deposits, and they undertook the internationalization of production.

Strategic partnerships facilitated the strong development of exploration and exploitation of hydrocarbons. Table III-8 presents investment figures for 1997, stemming from the various contracts that firms in Bolivia, Colombia and Venezuela signed, mainly with transnational firms.

With regard to the mining sector, CODELCO has benefited from Law 19,137, passed in 1992, which permits the company to form partnerships with third parties. The so-called CODELCO law has enabled the company to enter into strategic partnerships with foreign investors for the exploration and exploitation of hitherto unexploited mineral deposits. The company would not have been able to finance these projects on its own, and consequently the right to enter into partnerships has increased capacity. Partnerships currently represent over US$ 800 million of the corporation's assets, compared with only around US$ 15 million ten years ago (table III- 9).

Table III-8

PARTNERSHIP CONTRACTS BETWEEN STATE AND TRANSNATIONAL FIRMS IN HYDROCARBONS, 1997

COUNTRY	PARTNERSHIP CONTRACTS (MILLIONS OF DOLLARS)		
	EXPLORATION	EXPLOITATION	TOTAL
Bolivia	573	...	573
Colombia	335	1,183	1,518
Venezuela	...	12,000	12,000

Source: Authors' compilation based on information quoted in Humberto Campodónico, "La inversión en el sector petrolero peruano en le período 1993-2000", Reformas económicas series, No. 23 (LC/L.11207), Santiago, Chile, Economic Commission for Latin America and the Caribbean (ECLAC), 1999.

Table III-9

CODELCO PARTNERSHIPS WITH TRANSNATIONAL MINING COMPANIES

PROJECT	PARTNER	PRODUCT	NEGOTIATION
Exploitation contracts			
El Abra	Cyprus Amax (United States)	Copper	
Agua de la Falda	Homestake (United States)	Gold	
Exploration contracts			
Pastos Largos	MMAJ (Japan)	Copper	Current
Los Andes	AMP (Australia)	Copper	Current
El Loa	Asarco (United States)	Copper	Current
Inca de Oro	Rio Algom (Canada)	Copper, gold	In planning phase
Yabricoya	Cominco (Canada)	Copper	Current
Quebrada Valiente	Orvana/Helmo (Canada)	Gold	In planning phase
Manto Rojo	Cyprus Amax (United States)	Copper	In negotiation
Sierra Mariposa	Outokumpu (Finland)	Copper	In negotiation
Anillo	Several interested parties	Copper, gold	Bidding
San Antonio	Several interested parties	Copper	Bidding

Source: Corporación Nacional del Cobre de Chile (CODELCO-Chile), *Annual Report*, Santiago, Chile, 1997.

The internationalization of the exploration and exploitation of mineral and hydrocarbon deposits is a strategy to promote the discovery of new high-grade deposits now that national geological areas have largely been explored (this was the case for CODELCO at the end of the 1990s), or to find reserves in oil importing countries (PETROBRAS in Brazil and ENAP in Chile).

Large oil exporters, such as PDVSA and PEMEX, have focused their internationalization strategy on selling refined products on the international market. In Venezuela, strategic partnerships with foreign firms have enabled PDVSA to refine its oil surplus on several continents. In the 1990s, PEMEX followed this policy and entered the refining market in the United States.

As part of the internationalization policy, some State oil firms also designed strategies to penetrate the market for oil derivatives. In Brazil, PETROBRAS Internacional S.A. (BRASPETRO), a subsidiary of PETROBRAS, sells its products in Colombia, the United States and the United Kingdom. PDVSA has begun to break into the market through the firm Maraven, selling oil derivatives in Colombia, Ecuador and Peru.

In the natural gas sector, the sharp increase in reserves and regional production encouraged firms (State-owned, mixed and private) to develop gas transport infrastructure and to sell the product to neighbouring countries. Gas pipeline projects are currently underway between Argentina and Chile, Argentina and Brazil, Bolivia and Brazil, and Bolivia and Paraguay. The projects are part of a regional effort to bring about energy integration in Latin America.

Institutional reforms also promoted the adoption of new growth strategies among State-owned firms, including both the oil companies and the Chilean mining company (CODELCO). They were thus able to increase their investment levels substantially throughout the 1990s. Investment was further boosted by high liquidity levels in international capital markets, which gave the firms access to resources that were not available in previous decades (see table III-10).

Table III-10
INVESTMENT BY PUBLIC ENTERPRISES IN THE MINING AND HYDROCARBON SECTORS, 1990-1998
(millions of dollars)

FIRM	1990	1991	1992	1993	1994	1995	1996	1997	1998
PDVSA	3 472	4 192	4 405	4 598	4 766	5 089	5 372	n.a.	6 000
PEMEX	1 967	2 943	2 907	2 726	1 879	2 072	3 286	4 543	7 793
PETROBRAS	2 736	3 517	3 660	3 452	2 791	3 094	3 052	2 925	n.a.
ECOPETROL	311	312	493	698	790	1 059	1 433	1 518	n.a.
YPFB	100	105	108	70	72	35	40	n.a.	n.a.
CODELCO	331	343	425	402	341	365	702	853	600

Source: Authors' compilation from the database of the research project.

Transnational firms also increased their investment in the region, encouraged by new foreign investment laws, privatization, more flexible contractual arrangements, the deregulation of some markets (complete deregulation in the case of derivatives), price liberalization and the unrestricted availability of extracted crude oil. The reactivation of most economies in the region in the 1990s also helped to foster investment, as did the improved long-term growth prospects for the region. Together these elements stimulated the participation and repositioning of transnational corporations in the region's mining and hydrocarbon sectors.

These incentives also benefited domestic private firms that entered the sector. In oil and gas production, the most important firms include Bridas, Perez Companc, Pluspetrol and Astra in Argentina, and PBE Trading, Productos Industriales Venezolanos, Tecnoconsul, Hidropetrol and Servioil in Venezuela. The increased strength of these private and public companies boosted regional energy integration.

Deregulation and privatization gave rise to new microsectoral phenomena, including the integration of gas and electricity and of oil and gas. This integration is most prevalent in Argentina. As Gadano (1998) points out, the existence of a large gas supply at competitive prices makes the petrochemicals industry an attractive business both for hydrocarbon products and for large international petrochemical firms.

Thermoelectricity generation is another activity that contributed to the growth of natural gas production. In response to rising demand for electricity and a high level of obsolescence of the existing thermoelectric equipment in the region, gas producers entered the electricity market in Argentina, Bolivia, Brazil and Chile. The constant increase in electricity supply, which was partly due to the building of new plants, sparked a sharp fall in electricity prices. The number of thermoelectric projects underway in Argentina and Chile could actually cause an oversupply, especially if hydroelectricity enters another period of high production.

2. Types of Financing

Since the late 1980s, transnational mining and oil companies have forged investment partnerships and jointly carried out the exploitation of copper, gold and hydrocarbons, in particular. This is a marked contrast to the disputes between firms, especially in the copper industry, which were common in the early 1970s, when global competition for reserves was initiated. The current strategy has enabled firms to use their own capital to finance some of the investment necessary for exploitation, while the rest has come from partnerships between public firms, national capital, international investment societies and the World Bank. Tables III-11 and III-12 illustrate the partnerships involved in metal exploitation in Chile and Peru.

Table III-11
CHILE: TYPES OF FINANCING FOR MINING PROJECTS

PROJECT, BY REGION	PROJECT FINANCING	MILLIONS OF DOLLARS	DEVELOPMENT PERIOD
	REGION I		
Cerro Colorado	Contribution from partners: Río Algom, Canada	110	1992-1994
	Syndicated loan led by Citibank; sales contracts with the Mitsubishi agency	240	1997-1998
	(Japan) and KFW (Germany)	198	
Quebrada Blanca	Contribution from partners: Cominco, Teck Resources, Sociedad Minera	110	1993-1995
	Pudahuel and Enami	220	
	Group of banks led by Union Bank of Switzerland, Credit Lyonnais, and		
	Deutsche Bank		
Collahuasi	Contribution from partners: Minera Mantos Minorco and Falconbridge Ltda.,	1,500	1996-1998
	Japanese consortium 12% financing from international banks	200	
	REGION II		
El Abra	Contribution from partners: Codelco, Cyprus Amax; loan from international	1,050	1995-1997
	banks		
Mantos Blancos	Contribution from partners: Marvis Corp. (30%), Anglo American Corp.	160	1994-1996
	(13%), Somin (26%), Inversiones Sudamericanas (6.5%), other national		
	investors		
	Sale of shares in Proyecto Collahuasi for US$ 90 million		
El Lince	Contribution from partners: Grupo Luksic, Outokumpu, and Chemical Bank	60	1990-1992
Ivan y Zar	Contribution from partners: Rayrock Resources, Discovery Minera	36	1992-1994
Estefanía	Luksic	70	1993-1995

Table III-11 continued

PROJECT, BY REGION	PROJECT FINANCING	MILLIONS OF DOLLARS	DEVELOPMENT PERIOD
REGION II			
Tesoro/Leonor	Antofagasta Holdings (61%), Equatorial Treasure Ltd. (Australia) (39%) Project finance + sale of shares on stock market	75 175	1993-1995 1996-1997
Zaldívar	Outokumpu (50%), Placer Dome (50%)	750 28	1993-1995 1997
Lomas Bayas	Westmin – Canada Syndicated loan: BZW Mining Finance	110 140	1997-2000
Escondida	First expansion: Contribution from partners: BHP-UTAH, RTZ, Jeco, IFC + international loan + export credit	865 250 520 450 800	1993-1995 1994 1995-1996 1997-1998 1998
REGION III			
La Candelaria	Contribution from partners: Phelps Dodge (United States) and Sumitomo (Japan) Loans from financial institutions	1,620 337	1992-1995 1996-1998
REGION IV			
Los Pelambres	Antofagasta Holdings (60%) + Japanese consortia: Mitsubishi Material Corp (15%) and Nippon Mining & Metals (25%) + bank financing	400 935	1997-1998
METROPOLITAN REGION			
Los Bronces	Exxon Minerals International Inc. US	550 10	1991-1992 1997-1998

Source: Graciela Moguillansky, *La inversión en Chile: ¿el fin de un ciclo de expansión?*, Santiago, Chile, Economic Commission for Latin America and the Caribbean/Fondo de Cultura Económica, 1999.

Table III-12
PERU: INTERNATIONAL BANK FINANCING FOR MINING PROJECTS

COMPANY	PROJECT FINANCING	MILLIONS OF DOLLARS	DEVELOPMENT PERIOD
Southern Peru Copper Corporation (SPCC)	Eximbank (1996-2001) Mitsui & Co. Ltd. Bonds Banco de Crédito del Perú, Banco Continental, Banco Wiese Syndicated loan: Crédit Suisse, First Boston, Chase Securities, Deutsche Bank, Morgan Grenfell, Goldmann Sachs, JP Morgan Promissory notes backed by export guarantees	945	1997-2007
Cerro Verde	Banco de Crédito del Perú ABM AMRO Bank Chase Manhattan Bank of New York Citibank N.A. Banco Internacional del Perú	334.5	1997-2005
Yanacocha	Loan from International Finance Corporation (IFC) DEG loan Bank of New York-Salomon Brothers	155.3	
La Oroya	BT Alex-Brown-Donaldson, Lufkin & Jenrette Securities Corp. UBS Securities Banco de Crédito del Perú, Crédito Leasing S.A.	315	1998-2000 1998-2003 1998-2001 1999-2003
Refinería de Zinc Cajamarqilla	Lead Managers: Citicorp Securities, Inc., Bank of Montreal Export Development Corp. Banco de Crédito del Perú	250	1998-2002
Buenaventura	ADS (American Depository Shares). In US: ING Barings, JP Morgan, Salomon Brothers Barings-Nesbitt Burns, SBC Warburg	112	
Total		2112	

Source: Ministerio de Energía y Minas del Perú, taken from Humberto Campodónico, "Las reformas estructurales en el sector minero peruano y las características de la inversión 1992-2008", Reformas económicas series, No. 24 (LC/L.1209), Santiago, Chile, Economic Commission for Latin America and the Caribbean (ECLAC), 1999.

In Chile –where most of the region's mining projects were carried out in the 1990s– statistics from the Foreign Investment Committee indicate that between 30% and 40% of the capital was put up by the partners themselves, with the rest coming from syndicated loans from international commercial banks. In addition, a lower percentage was often financed through long-term purchasing contracts, particularly in the case of mineral concentrates.

Unlike their Chile counterparts, mining firms in Peru not only financed part of their projects on the international market, but also borrowed actively in the domestic financial market. Oil companies in Argentina did the same. In the Argentine hydrocarbon sector, the use of tradable debt instruments was very widespread. The number of operations increased considerably, reaching US$ 2.13 billion in 1997. Resources were also obtained on the stock market, where the stocks of YPF, Cadipsa, Capex and Compañía General de Combustibles (CGC) are traded.

The opening of the capital account, financial liberalization and sectoral reform policies enabled these firms to overcome the difficulties of raising investment funds for large projects. However, as a result of the international financial crisis, which began in Asia and then worsened with the Russian collapse, loans were frozen, particularly for mining, and prices fell sharply. Many firms were in the process of raising funds for various projects, and they suffered considerable setbacks.

E. CAPITAL FORMATION AND SECTORAL PERFORMANCE

A number of positive elements combined in the 1990s to foster investment in mining and hydrocarbons, but the projects will only materialize in the future. According to sectoral information, Chile accounted for 67% of the region's investment in mining over the past decade. Brazil came second with 19%, followed by Peru and Argentina (tables III-13 and III-14). Three factors contributed to investment growth in the sector: institutional changes, which opened up new investment opportunities for transnational firms; the shift of the world market toward higher-value minerals; and strong international liquidity, which provided large volumes of investment.

In the case of Chile, the level of investment shown in the table represents the peak of a 15 year sectoral investment cycle which began in the 1980s and which should end around 2000. In the 1970s, issues related to the institutional framework (for example, new foreign investment laws and the mining law) were key in attracting foreign investors to Chile and particularly to mining exploration. These factors were not enough to stimulate projects, however. Investment did not take off until a decade later, with the Escondida project in

Table III-13
INVESTMENT IN MINING, 1990-1998
(*millions of dollars*)

COUNTRY	CUMULATIVE TOTAL 1990-1998	ANNUAL AVERAGE
Argentina	2 288	381
Chile	15 505	1 723
Brazil	4 436	493
Peru	2 925	418

Source: Authors' compilation from the database of the research project.

Table III-14
INVESTMENT IN MINING AS A PERCENTAGE OF GDP, 1990-1997

COUNTRY	1990	1991	1992	1993	1994	1995	1996	1997
Argentina	...	...	...	0.01	0.03	0.06	0.27	0.24
Brazil	0.09	0.10	0.10	0.03	0.08	0.07	0.08	0.08
Chile	3.91	2.54	2.62	3.95	5.41	4.00	3.97	3.90
Peru	0.16	0.08	0.05	0.19	0.43	0.86	0.74	0.83

Source: Authors' compilation from the database of the research project.

the late 1980s. Financing for the project was restricted at first by the difficulties in the international financial market.[26]

In the 1990s, Chile benefited from the high levels of liquidity in international capital markets, and was consequently able to finance mega-projects. This positive environment also enabled Argentina and Peru to create the conditions for sectoral development and to attract foreign capital. In Peru investment began to recover from a period of stagnation, thanks to the 1992

---

26   See Moguillansky (1998b) on the development of investment in the Chilean mining sector.

institutional reform and to the process of privatizing public mining companies. Privatization forced the firms to make investment commitments to increase exploitation, smelting and refining. Later, an aggressive exploration programme was promoted. New technical and legal measures fostered the rapid growth in the number of hectares under mining exploration, which rose from 10 million to 17 million hectares. Companies such as RTZ, Asarco, Newmont, Phelps Dodge and Cyprus Amax carried out the exploitation.

In Argentina, institutional reform and the positive international market for minerals in the 1990s attracted foreign direct investment flows to the sector. Inflows grew from US$ 2 million in 1992 to US$ 316 million in 1996. This increase coincided with the establishment of several important foreign firms in the country, which carried out prospecting, exploration and, in some cases, the exploitation of new mineral deposits.

Table III-15 lists the projects that will potentially be developed over the next few years in Argentina, Chile and Peru. In most cases, the implementation of the projects will depend on the evolution of the world mineral market. At the moment, the copper situation is very uncertain, as the international price has been well below the long-term price considered profitable for the business. The closure of low-grade mines should foster the sector's recovery in the medium term.

Brazil is the only one of the four countries in which mining investment stagnated in the 1990s. The sector developed very differently from that in other countries, largely because of the poor performance of the international market for Brazil's traditional minerals, low levels of exploration and lack of geological data on the vast country, the strategy of State-owned CVRD which pushed rationalization and the discovery of new reserves over the expansion of productive capacity, and the high cost of infrastructure for mineral production in the Amazon.

Evaluating the performance of investment in hydrocarbons is more complex than for mining (table III-16). Institutional reforms stimulated exploration, with recovery evident in all the countries which implemented reforms, but exploration did not always lead to the discovery of economically exploitable reserves. In addition, although figures on investment are available (table III-17), it is not possible to evaluate how well the policies have worked given the short time that has elapsed since the reforms were implemented. (Table III-18 shows data on the physical volume of oil production.) In many cases, new firms are still in the exploration stage, when investment levels are much lower than those associated with production and industrial development. However, microeconomic analysis can provide more data on the investment behaviour of private firms.

Table III-15
PROJECTS IN THE PIPELINE FOR 2001 TO 2007

PROJECT	INVESTOR	METAL	INVESTMENT IN MILLIONS DOLLARS
CHILE			
Spence	Río Algom, Canada	Copper	500
Los Bronces y las Tórtolas	Exxon Minerals International Inc. US.	Copper	550
San Antonio	Codelco and private bidding (60 ó 95% of the shares)	Copper	250
Tuina	Yuma Copper Corp., Canada	Copper	30
Relincho	Outokumpu-Equatorial	Copper	200
Santa Catalina	Cía. Minera Santa Catalina S.A.	Copper	100
Ivan y Zar	Rayrock Resources Ltda. and Discovery Minera	Copper	36
Aldebarán/Cerro Casale	Placer Dome, Arizona Star, Bema Gold	Gold	1,300
Refinería de cobre	Acec Union Miniere, Belgium, 20% Brasil Arbi Participaçoes	Copper	500
Fundición de cobre	Hyundai	Copper	400
ARGENTINA			
El Pachón	Cambior Inc. y Companía Minera San José	Copper-gold	800
Agua Rica	Northern Orion Exploration y BHP Copper	Copper-gold	500
Potasio Río Colorado	Grupo Minera Tea – Cra	Potassium	150
San Jorge	Northern Orion Exploration	Copper-gold	110
PERU			
Antamina	Río Algom, Noranda Teck	Copper	1,064
Cuajone	Southern Peru Copper Corp.	Copper	499
Cerro Verde	Cyprus Amax	Copper	50
Doe Run Perú	Doe Run	Copper	166
Cajamarquilla	Cominco y Marubeni	Zinc	20

Source: Authors' compilation from the database of the research project

Table III-16

PERFORMANCE INDICATORS IN THE MINING SECTOR, 1970-1998

INDICATOR AND COUNTRY	1970	1980	1990	1997	1998
		EXPORTS IN MILLIONS OF DOLLARS			
Argentina	8	174	302	407	699
Brazil	277	1 894	4 257	4 913	4 975
Chile	1 066	2 900	4 489	7 792	6 211
Peru	505	1 499	1 558	2 403	1 985
		EXPORT INDEX 1990 = 100			
Argentina	3	58	100	135	231
Brazil	6	44	100	115	117
Chile	24	65	100	174	138
Peru	32	96	100	154	127
		PHYSICAL VOLUME OF PRODUCTION 1990 = 100			
Brazil	27	68	100	120	n.a.
Chile	74	82	100	169	n.a.
Peru	133	120	100	147	n.a.

Source: Foreign Trade Database of Latin America and the Caribbean (Banco de Datos del Comercio Exterior de América Latina y el Caribe, BADACEL), Economic Commission for Latin America and the Caribbean (ECLAC); *Statistical Yearbook for Latin America and the Caribbean*, Santiago, Chile, various issues.

Table III-17

INVESTMENT COEFFICIENT IN THE HYDROCARBON
SECTOR, 1988-1997
(percent)

COUNTRY	1988	1990	1991	1992	1993	1994	1995	1996	1997
Bolivia	2.56	3.20	3.92	3.56	2.84	2.95	2.86	2.41	n.a.
Brazil	n.a.	0.48	0.55	0.57	0.50	0.41	0.44	0.40	0.38
Colombia	1.12	1.13	1.22	1.98	1.26	2.05	1.70	1.67	1.61
Mexico	0.80	0.73	0.92	0.79	0.67	0.69	0.78	0.94	1.04
Peru	0.50	0.23	0.21	0.18	0.25	0.23	0.21	n.a.	n.a.

Source: Authors' compilation from the database of the research project.

Table III-18
INDEX OF THE PHYSICAL VOLUME OF OIL PRODUCTION, 1970-1997
(1990 = 100)

COUNTRY	1970	1980	1990	1991	1992	1993	1994	1995	1996	1997
Argentina	81	102	100	102	115	123	138	149	157	167
Bolivia	116	109	100	106	102	106	123	136	140	143
Brazil	26	29	100	99	100	101	105	109	124	133
Colombia	50	29	100	97	100	103	103	133	143	135
Mexico	20	83	100	105	105	105	105	103	112	117
Peru	56	152	100	89	90	98	99	94	93	92

Source: Economic Commission for Latin America and the Caribbean (ECLAC), *Statistical Yearbook for Latin America and the Caribbean*, Santiago, Chile, various issues.

The case of Argentina illustrates how firms behaved after privatization. Oil and gas reserves grew jointly with production, maintaining a horizon of between 9 and 10 years (Gadano, 1998). YPF, which by 1998 accounted for approximately 43% of oil production and 34% of gas production, invested an average of US$ 1.9 billion per year in expanding capital for upstream activities (both domestically and abroad) and for downstream activities. According to Gadano's data, US$ 7.25 billion was invested in the oil and gas derivatives industry between 1990 and 1997, thereby increasing the share of these products in hydrocarbon exports.

Since 1997, the capitalization of the Bolivian State hydrocarbon company has led to investment commitments of US$ 4.3 billion in the space of eight years. This investment involves new areas of exploration and exploitation, including partnerships with other countries –particularly with Petrobras– and the construction of the gas pipeline between Bolivia and Brazil. This will enable a marked increase in exports, which should rise from the current 10% of total exports to 35%. The total should rise even more once the project to build a new gas pipeline between Santa Cruz (Bolivia) and Cuibá (Brazil) is finished.

Colombia traditionally was not a large oil exporter, but in the last decade the discovery of sizeable reserves made it an important producer. Most exploration and development was carried out via partnership contracts with the State company, given that the terms of these contracts improved the situation for foreign investment (Fainboim and Rodríguez, 2000).

In Mexico the State is legally required to retain control over oil. The economic consequence is that most investment decisions to date have been based on macroeconomic factors, which are frequently short-term, which override microeconomic considerations and which limit financing of the industry. Private investment in the sector has been meagre, while public investment has recovered significantly since the end of the tequila crisis (Torres, 1999).

Investment in the Brazilian oil sector performed modestly in the 1990s, both in absolute terms and as a proportion of GDP. This was partially due to previous investment levels and partially to the financial constraints faced by Petrobras.

In Peru sectoral reform is also in its early stages, and its effect on investment is still quite small. However, starting in 1993, the State firm Petroperú signed 37 licensing contracts for hydrocarbon exploration, which brought in investment of US$ 1.27 billion dollars over seven years. In the case of oil discovery, private firms will make the investments necessary to develop production. Of the wells explored to date, not one has registered enough oil to make exploitation commercially feasible.

Insufficient time has passed for assessing private investor behaviour in the hydrocarbon sector. However, foreign participation in exploration, the acquisition of State enterprises and strategic partnerships with firms that remain in the State sector are all good indicators of strong future investment growth in the sector.

CHAPTER IV

INVESTMENT IN INFRASTRUCTURE

A country's infrastructure is composed of a number of specific sectors, such as electricity, telecommunications, rural and urban roads, sewage and water supply, irrigation, ports and airports. This study concentrates on the first three sectors, because of the advances made in these areas as a result of the reforms and their importance to productive growth and international competitiveness.[27]

Despite differences in the services offered and in the characteristics of the respective markets, the reform process has been similar in the electricity and telecommunications sectors, allowing them to be analysed together. Roads are addressed in a separate section. The nature of the latter activity required a new form of private sector participation –concessions–, which became widespread in the region in the 1990s.

A. THE NEW INSTITUTIONAL FRAMEWORK IN ELECTRICITY AND TELECOMMUNICATIONS

The main objective of the reform process in electricity and telecommunications has been to include the private sector in the ownership, management and generation of infrastructure services. In general, the first

---

27 The information contained in the text, tables, boxes and figures in this chapter, which come from this study's database, are taken from the following authors or bibliographical references: Barja (1999b, 1999c); Bielschowsky (1999b); Campodónico (1999a, 1999d); Celani (1998); Cordero (2000); Delgado (1998); Escobar (1999); Fainboim and Rodríguez (2000); Moguillansky (1997a, 1997b, 1998a); Romero (1998); Rodríguez (1999); Scheinver (1999).

step towards achieving this goal was the creation of an institutional framework to serve as the basis for privatization.

The electricity and telecommunications sectors were deeply transformed in the 1990s. Previously, public service State monopolies –limited by a centralized structure, with vertically integrated markets– were concerned mainly with guaranteeing supply and creating positive externalities, and they operated in a framework in which pricing policy was not designed to maximize profits. The government often prioritized distributive and inflation-controlling criteria, while management did not always follow cost-minimizing policies. The foreign debt crisis, the scarcity of financial resources and the pressure exerted by multinational organizations such as the International Monetary Fund and the World Bank forced sectoral reform.

There followed a radical change, which led to the privatization of public utilities or the award of long-term concessions, changes in industrial organization and market structure, the introduction of new rules of the game, and new legislation and regulatory institutions.

The participation of the private sector and the new institutional framework changed the way investment decisions are made. This chapter evaluates the changes and analyses whether the development of public services can be better executed in this new context than under the logic of the public sector.

The level of private sector participation in infrastructure activities remains uneven between countries, and outcomes are not yet definitive. In some countries privatization was carried out before changes in legislation and the rules of the game were introduced, whereas in others the sequence was reversed. The sequence of these processes is significant because once the terms of purchase have been negotiated with the companies in question, it is difficult to change them retroactively. Any change in the regulation of a particular sector causes great uncertainty among investors, which in turn can threaten the level of investment.

1.   The Privatization Process

The political, macroeconomic and international context in which the companies were sold determined the type of participants involved and the commitments negotiated between the public and private sectors. An example of this is the contrast between the privatization of the large public utilities in Chile in the mid-1980s and the experience five or ten years later in Bolivia, Brazil, Colombia or Peru.

Indeed, Chile was the first country in the region to privatize these companies, and the process was carried out when the domestic and regional economies were going through a major crisis. The new policies and mechanisms that emerged were crucial to the success of the process, because they managed to attract private sector participation. The new policies included measures to guarantee higher profits and reduce uncertainty. They included the following: (a) the modernization of the management structure and the write-off of firms' debts before privatization; (b) a new tariff regime, set several years before the sale, which guaranteed a high return on investment; and (c) other incentives designed to encourage firms to invest in the new business, such as subsidized shares and loans, new mechanisms –again involving subsidies– which enabled public sector employees to acquire controlling stakes in the companies, and a new institutional framework that initially spurred investment, although it was subsequently perceived as obstructing the healthy development of the sector. With the exception of Argentina, which also began privatization relatively early, the other countries initiated the process in the second half of the 1990s in a context of economic stability and abundant international liquidity. As illustrated in table IV-1, much of the process was carried out before the Asian crisis. These conditions, together with the success of the Chilean experience in terms of the growth and profitability of the companies, attracted the participation of foreign investors. Acting in consortia and backed by international financing, European, North American and Chilean firms took over the companies (see table A-8 in the annex).

The negotiations between the State and investors in the 1990s helped overcome some of the deficiencies in existing regulations and corrected some of the errors committed during the pioneering Chilean process. In some cases this allowed the government to maximize its revenue from the sale of the companies or created incentives for subsequent investment.

2. Market Structure

Even though the privatization process was designed to create competitive markets, the tendency towards mergers and the concentration of ownership – encouraged by the lack of anti-trust legislation– quickly gave rise to oligopolies markets.

The way in which State enterprises were privatized shaped the structure of the post-reform market. In general, two trends occurred in each of the sectors studied. In the electricity sector the company was "deverticalized", and separate markets were created for generation, distribution, transmission and, in some countries, commercialization (see table IV-2). Although the markets for generation and commercialization can both work well under competitive conditions, in the case of generation competition tends to be restricted or oligopolistic. In the case of distribution and transmission markets, it is not economically feasible to have more than one company operating in each geographical area. In the telecommunications sector, by contrast, the trend was to preserve the vertical integration of the company, giving the private operator a long period of monopoly rights.

Table IV-1

SECTORAL REFORM AND THE PRIVATIZATION PROCESS

REFORM OF ELECTRICITY SECTOR	PRIVATIZATION OF ELECTRICITY SECTOR
ARGENTINA	
Law 23,696 of 1989	1992: Sale of share packages Provincial firms from 1995 Atomic energy (underway) Binational hydroelectric plants (underway)
BOLIVIA	
Reform process (1994)	1995: Capitalization of generating companies 1995: Bidding for distribution company Elfec 1997: Sale of transmission company
BRAZIL	
Law 8,631 and Decree 774 March 1993	Law 9,074 of 1995: sale of local distributor firms Law 8,987 of 1995: independent electricity production
COLOMBIA	
Laws 142 and 143, 1994: Competition in generation Creation of wholesale market	1995-1997: Sale of share packages in generating companies
CHILE	
1982 General law of electricity services 1982 Reform of price system	1986-1989: Sale of generating, distribution and transmission companies
MEXICO	
1989: Start of restructuring of public enterprise 1992: Redefinition of public services and modification of public service law for electricity	Not privatized

Table IV-1 continued

	REFORM OF TELECOMMUNICATIONS SECTOR	PRIVATIZATION OF TELECOMMUNICATIONS SECTOR
PERU	DI 674, 1991: Constitution of Copri	1994: Sale of generating, distribution, and transmission companies
ARGENTINA	Reform Law No. 23,696, 1989 Decree 731/89	1990: Sale of shares in Entel to two basic telephone operators; constitution of geographical monopolies
BOLIVIA	Telecommunications Law 1995: Capitalization of Entel Exclusive concession for basic telephone service co-operatives	Entel monopoly on national long distance and international calls Regional monopolies in basic telephone services Duopoly in cellular telephone service
BRAZIL	1995: Constitutional amendment No.8 1996-1997: Cellular telephone law General telecommunications law	1997: Privatization of Telebras Opening of cellular telephone market Creation of competition through "mirror" firms in regional markets for basic and long distance services
COLOMBIA	1989: Opening of new private concessions 1990: Local telephone service regulation	1994: competition in local telephone service 1993: introduction of mobile cellular telephones 1998: introduction of competition in long distance service
CHILE	1982: General telecommunications law 1994: Reforms to the law: Introduction of multi-carrier system	1990-1994: Vertically segmented markets in local and long distance services for Entel and CTC Free entry for new competitors to all products 1994 all markets open to competition

Table IV-1 continued

REFORM OF TELECOMMUNICATIONS SECTOR	PRIVATIZATION OF TELECOMMUNICATIONS SECTOR
MEXICO	
1995: Federal telecommunications Law 1997: Competition in national long distance and international calls	1990: Privatization of Telmex Monopoly in basic and long distance services 1997: Opening to competition in all market segments
PERU	
New telecommunications Law	Private monopoly 1999: competition introduced

Source: Authors' compilation from the database of the research project.

Table IV-2
STRUCTURE OF THE ELECTRICITY AND TELECOMMUNICATIONS MARKETS

ELECTRICITY SECTOR	TELECOMMUNICATIONS SECTOR
	ARGENTINA
Vertical break-up into generation, transport and distribution	Definition of an exclusivity period in two geographical monopolies for basic phone services
Horizontal separation of generating companies	Cellular market shared between Telefónica and Telecom
Competitive market for generation with low minimum entry thresholds: 40 firms	Competition in new service segments (1998)
Transmission companies: 6 monopoly firms (benefiting from economies of scale)	Competition in mobile phones, cable TV and other areas
Distribution companies: 25 firms, legal monopolies with potential competition	
	BOLIVIA
Separation of generation, transport and distribution	Continued Entel monopoly in national and international long distance service
Limit on potential generation capacity per firm: 35% of the market	Continued regional monopolies for basic services
Creation of wholesale market in generation: 4 firms with exclusive rights until 1999	Duopoly in cellular market
Creation of 6 distribution firms, regional monopolies	
	BRAZIL
Generation: State run, in process of privatization	1997: Opening of cellular telephone market
Transmission: 100% State-run; Electrobras and State firms being prepared for privatization	1998: Incorporation of 9 mobile telephone operators
Distribution: privatization of State monopolies 1995-1998	Three private regional monopolies in basic telephone services
Decree 1,009 de 1993:	Duopoly in long distance service
Open access to federal transmission network	Opening to competition in basic telephone services from new operators in each region.
Open access to distribution	
	COLOMBIA
Vertical integration in large firms	38 local telephone companies, of which 4 cover 84% of installed lines
Private ownership of 50% of generation and 30% of distribution	Three regional duopolies in cellular services
Generation: 23 private and 13 public sector firms	From 1998 competition in long distance calls, and competition in value added services
Commercialization: 35 public and 39 private firms	
Transmission: 8 public and 3 private firms	
Distribution: 34 public and 3 private firms	

Table IV-2 continued

ELECTRICITY SECTOR	TELECOMMUNICATIONS SECTOR
CHILE	
Vertical integration in generation and transmission	1989–1993: Vertically segmented markets maintained for local telephone service in hands of Entel and CTC
Interconnected Central System (ICS):	Free entry to all competitors for new services
Oligopoly in generation	1994: Opening to competition of all markets
Distribution: 10 firms (private monopolies)	
Northern Interconnected Central System (NICS):	
Generation: strong competition since introduction of gas pipelines	
Distribution: 3 regional firms (monopolies)	
MEXICO	
State monopoly:	1990-1997: Definition of an exclusivity period for a private monopoly
Generation: 94.3% State, 5.7% private	1998: Opening to competition
Transmission and distribution: 100% State	
PERU	
Separation of generating, transmission and distribution activities	Private vertically integrated monopoly
Generation:	Introduction of competition in 1999
51% private (5 firms)	
49% State (3 firms)	
Distribution:	
3 firms, regional private monopolies	
6 public sector regional firms	

Source: Authors' compilation from the database of the research project.

It is worth noting that the trend toward mergers and acquisitions of companies by international operators has led to a situation in which markets that were vertically disintegrated at the time of privatization or which were opened up to competition by subsequent legislation have once again become vertically integrated, especially when there was no legislation to prevent this. This situation is found in the electricity and telecommunications sectors of more than one country in the region.[28]

In other cases, the legislation allowed new entrants into the market, but sunk costs were prohibitive in practice. This is evident in basic telephone services characterized by a dominant operator, and in the market for generation when electricity plants are grouped into a single company rather than being separated horizontally under different ownership. Nevertheless, technological progress in both telecommunications (mobile telephones) and the electricity sector (plants with combined cycles) has allowed products and services to be developed at much lower costs and has consequently fostered competition. Table IV-3 summarizes the current structure of both sectors.

3. Regulation

One of the negatives in this post-reform transition stage is the weakness of supervision and regulation, which is evident in all of the countries studied. The characteristics of the regulatory framework shape future investment in two ways: (a) by fostering competition and maintaining a separation between companies that could be vertically and horizontally linked, and (b) by facilitating the negotiation of the pricing structure in the regulated market, which fosters investment while allowing the consumer to benefit from any productivity gains.

a. Promotion of Competition

While there is no consensus in economic theory about the real effect of competition on innovation and investment, its influence has clearly had a positive effect on technological progress. Fierce competition in telecommunications at the global level has led to a degree of technological progress not experienced in other sectors. It also led the transnational corporations in the Latin American market to push for innovation and to introduce new services and products to strengthen their position when the telecommunications market was opened.

---

28   See Moguillansky (1997b, 1998a) and Campodónico (1999a).

Table IV- 3
DEGREE OF MARKET COMPETITION IN ELECTRICITY AND TELECOMMUNICATIONS

ELECTRICITY SECTOR	GENERATION	DISTRIBUTION	TRANSMISSION
	Potential competition Oligopoly in practice	Private monopoly	State or private monopoly
TELECOMMUNICATIONS SECTOR	BASIC TELEPHONE SERVICE	MOBILE TELEPHONE SERVICE	LONG DISTANCE SERVICE
	Private monopoly Potential competition	Potential competition Competitive market in some countries	Potential competition Competitive market in Chile, and recently in other countries

Source: Authors' compilation from the database of the research project.

The Chilean experience is a good example of how telecommunications companies behaved after the market was opened up to competition. The introduction of a multi-carrier system for long distance services and the liberalization of other segments of the market benefited the country not only because they triggered the introduction of new technology and competitiveness, but also because competition led to an extraordinary reduction in the prices of products and services, which was not the case in other countries. At the moment, the major obstacle to future sectoral growth is the trend for the largest company to merge with or acquire the other companies when anti-monopoly legislation is not fully developed.

In Colombia, there is a similar situation in basic telephone services: the free entry of new operators in a structure of decentralized networks paved the way for competition in a segment of the market that is monopolistic in the majority of countries. The same also occurs in the market for electricity generation. In Colombia and Argentina, not only has competition allowed prices to fall dramatically in the free market to which the largest consumers have access, but it has also secured the supply and increased the quality of services.

b.   The Pricing Regime

The pricing regime reflects the structure of regulated markets in the wake of privatization. These are markets with no potential for competition (see table IV-4), and a regulatory body periodically negotiates the prices charged by the natural monopolies. In market segments which do have potential for competition, the price tends to be determined by supply and demand, without State intervention.

Table IV-4
REGULATED MARKETS IN THE ELECTRICITY AND TELECOMMUNICATIONS SECTORS

ELECTRICITY SECTOR	TELECOMMUNICATIONS SECTOR
Generation (Consumption below 0.5, 1 or 2 MW, depending on the limit fixed in each country)	Basic telephone service
Transmission	Long distance service (Except in countries where the market is open to competition)
Distribution	Mobile telephone service (From 1998, in Chile)

Source: Authors' compilation from the database of the research project.

There are several ways in which prices are set in regulated markets in different countries, both in the electricity sector and in telecommunications. In the former, these formulae are based on models with parameters negotiated with the companies. Although the pricing model can be the same in different cases, the parameters are not necessarily the same. In general, the prices are set to incorporate the cost of operation, maintenance, reserves, and expansion or new investments; some countries also take into account a minimum return on investment (in Bolivia 9%, in Chile 10% and in Peru 12%). Other countries introduced a system of price capping, which was based on prices in developed countries and was set for a fixed period of time (see table A-10 in the annex). Still others (Argentina) included efficiency considerations in the parameters used to set prices, thus making prices subject to certain quality objectives and to periodic revisions, after which future price reductions were set as a function of the productivity and efficiency levels achieved.

In the telecommunications sector, State companies were privatized without establishing a pricing regime, which caused subsequent difficulties when the regulatory body tried to change the rules of the game. In those countries where the corresponding legislation was not approved, prices have remained high, cross-subsidies have prevailed and the regulatory bodies have struggled to reduce prices in line with efficiency and productivity gains. Companies which combine accounting records for related services make the task even more difficult.

Bolivia, Chile and Colombia established pricing models that were rather more transparent (see table A-11 in the annex). Among these countries, Chile is the only one that has already undergone negotiations between the regulatory body and the monopoly in basic telephone services. After intense discussions, the regulatory body succeed in getting the dominant company to reduce its prices in line with productivity gains.

The pricing model in regulated markets determines the profitability of companies. Using the accounts of these companies, it is possible to calculate the profitability achieved after privatization. The results obtained show that (a) the profitability of the sector is quite high in most countries, which explains why international firms are keen to enter the region; (b) in the case of Chile, despite the price cuts agreed every four years the basic telephone service company (Companía de Telecomunicaciones de Chile, CTC) has managed to expand its business in non-regulated markets and increase its profitability by becoming a universal provider; and (c) also in Chile, when the Empresa Nacional de Telecomunicaciones (ENTEL) was privatized, it was the only long distance service provider, but profits fell sharply when competitors entered this segment of the market –eight companies currently operate in the sector– and ENTEL was forced to expand its business into other markets (see table IV-5).

Table IV-5
PROFITABILITY OF PRIVATIZED FIRMS IN THE TELECOMMUNICATIONS SECTOR[a], 1991-1997

COUNTRY	FIRM	1991	1992	1993	1994	1995	1996	1997
Argentina	TELECOM + TELEFÓNICA: Monopoly in entire market	4.0	9.0	12.0	16.0	19.0	17.0	25.0
Chile	CTC: Monopoly in basic market until 1994	15.1	17.5	20.0	16.9	15.8	20.4	20.0
	ENTEL: Monopoly in long distance market until 1994	47.9	47.8	48.2	36.5	16.9	2.3	4.8
Bolivia	ENTEL: Monopoly in long distance market	n.a.	n.a.	5.8	8.1	3.2	6.1	6.2
Mexico	TELMEX: Monopoly in entire market	26.1	24.3	22.7	13.1	11.3	13.0	14.5
Peru	TELEFÓNICA DEL PERÚ: Monopoly in entire market	n.a.	n.a.	n.a.	2.9	21.1	20.8	20.8

Source: Authors' compilation from the database of the research project.
a/ Measured as net profits as share of assets.

B. INVESTMENT AFTER THE REFORMS IN ELECTRICITY AND TELECOMMUNICATIONS

An evaluation of sectoral and particularly investment performance in the post-reform period should take into account the specific characteristics of the period and the fact that not much time has elapsed since the reforms took place. The bulk of privatizations occurred in the second half of the 1990s, which makes it impossible to reach a definitive conclusion about the process. Moreover, an important share of the investments was determined by transitory factors that will no longer apply once the sectoral reforms have been consolidated (see table IV-6). Rather than evaluate the figures, therefore, we aim to show the series of factors that spurred investment and the factors that will shape future sectoral development.

1. Transitory Factors that Determined Sectoral Investment

a. Pent-up Demand in Telecommunications

In the telecommunications sector, investors, especially international firms, were attracted by the very high levels of pent-up demand, as well as the outdated technology and low productivity levels that prevailed in the region. At the time of privatization, there was a severe shortage of telephone lines and technology was outdated. These two factors explain the strong investment in all the countries, which is reflected in the investment-to-GDP ratios (see table IV-7).

In the electricity sector, by contrast, supply was practically universal at the time of privatization in most countries, at least in urban areas, so there was virtually no pent-up demand in the sector. In some countries, like Chile and Argentina, the abundance of energy reserves and previous State investment explain the lower investment ratios after privatizations. In the case of Argentina, the large hydroelectric projects at Chocón, Cerros Colorados, Piedra de Águila and Yaciretá, together with the nuclear plants, provided enough supply to last for several years. This did not hold back private sector participation, however, which was concentrated on thermoelectric energy generation (combined cycle plants) and distribution; investment in these segments was very dynamic.[29] Lower costs resulting from technological

---

29   Between 1993 and 1997 this gave rise to an expansion of 2,300 MW in the country, and an additional 4,500 MW were approved for two new plants and expansion at existing facilities, which were expected to go ahead between 1998 and 2000. The private sector has also played an active role in distribution, investing the equivalent of US$ 284 million annually.

Table IV-6
TEMPORARY FACTORS INFLUENCING INVESTMENT IN ELECTRICITY AND TELECOMMUNICATIONS

COUNTRY	ELECTRICITY SECTOR				TELECOMMUNICATIONS SECTOR			
	PRE-REFORM RESERVES AND SUPPLY	INVESTMENT COMMITMENTS FOR EXPANSION OF QUALITY IMPROVEMENTS	STATE PARTICIPATION IN INVESTMENT	PRICE INCENTIVES AND OTHER FORMS OF INCENTIVES	PRE-REFORM RESERVES AND SUPPLY	INVESTMENT COMMITMENTS FOR EXPANSION OF QUALITY IMPROVEMENTS	STATE PARTICIPATION IN INVESTMENT	PRICE INCENTIVES AND OTHER FORMS OF INCENTIVES
Argentina	Large generating reserves. Lack of maintenance in distribution and transmission	Commitment with fines imposed if not met	Medium		Large shortage	Yes	No	Maintenance of cross-subsidy
Bolivia	Large generating reserves	Investment commitment	None	Minimum profitability of 9% over the expansion of fixed assets	Large shortage	Yes	No	Fixing of initial high prices
Brazil	Shortages in generation and distribution		High		Large shortage. Previous State investment	Yes	No	Fixing of initial high prices
Colombia	Shortage in generation. Regional distribution companies insolvent	Quality commitment from 1998	Medium	State guarantee to buy the service	Large shortage	Yes	No	Fixing of initial high tariff. Subsidies for low income sectors
Chile	Moderate generating reserves	None	None	Minimum profitability 10% on expansion of fixed assets	Large shortage	No	No	Minimum profitability 10% on expansion of fixed assets

Table IV-2 continued

Country	Electricity sector				Telecommunications sector			
	Pre-reform reserves and supply	Investment commitments for expansion of quality improvements	State participation in investment	Price incentives and other forms of incentives	Pre-reform reserves and supply	Investment commitments for expansion of quality improvements	State participation in investment	Price incentives and other forms of incentives
Mexico	State monopoly				Large shortage	Yes	No	Fixing of initial high prices
Peru	Shortage in generation	Commitment to invest in generation	Medium	Minimum profitability 12% on expansion of fixed assets	Large shortage	Yes	No	Maintenance of cross-subsidy

Source: Authors' compilation from the database of the research project.

Table IV-7
INVESTMENT IN THE ELECTRICITY AND
TELECOMMUNICATIONS SECTORS, 1980-1997
(Percentage of GDP)

	1980-1988	1989	1990-1995	1997
ELECTRICITY SECTOR				
Argentina	1.3	0.5	0.4	0.3
Bolivia	n.a.	0.8	1.5	2.3
Brazil	1.6	1.7	1.1	0.6
Colombia	2.4	1.7	2.2	2.6
Costa Rica	1.9	n.a.	1.8	2.6
Chile	1.7	2.0	1.3	2.1
Mexico	n.a.	0.6	0.6	n.a.
Peru	1.4	0.4	1.1	1.2
TELECOMMUNICATIONS SECTOR				
Argentina	n.a.	n.a.	0.7	n.a.
Bolivia	n.a.	n.a.	0.7	2.3
Brazil	0.4	0.6	0.6	0.8
Colombia	0.4	0.5	0.7	1.4
Costa Rica	n.a.	n.a.	n.a.	n.a.
Chile	0.6	0.6	1.3	1.9
Mexico	n.a.	0.4	0.5	0.2
Peru	0.1	0.1	1.1	0.8

Source: Authors' compilation from the database of the research project.

progress in machinery, equipment and infrastructure also explain the lower levels of investment. In Chile, the State generator, Empresa Nacional de Electricidad S.A. (ENDESA), carried out large hydroelectric projects before privatization, but afterwards the private sector had to continue to raise investment to meet the demand created by rapid economic growth.[30]

b.   Investment, Expansion and Modernization Commitments

The investment, expansion and modernization commitments taken on by the investors when they acquired controlling stakes in the companies were an important factor in spurring investment in the period after privatization.

---

30   Since the privatization process was completed in Chile in 1989, the rate of investment has accelerated strongly, reaching double the average annual levels observed in the 1980s. Annual investment of 1.5% of GDP in the 1990s has allowed the electricity supply to expand at a sufficient rate to satisfy the growth in demand for electricity consumption at a rate of 7.5% of GDP.

Two types of instruments spurred investment, and they are related to the way in which the controlling stakes in the companies were made available in the 1990s. The first led to direct investment commitments, as was the case in Bolivia through the capitalization mechanism.[31] The second type of instrument required the company to carry out projects within a period fixed at the time of the sale, as occurred in Peru. Table IV-8 shows the required investments, based on the most conservative assumptions of demand growth.

Table IV-8
INVESTMENT COMMITMENTS IN CAPITALIZED AND PRIVATIZED FIRMS IN PERU AND BOLIVIA IN ELECTRICITY AND TELECOMMUNICATIONS
(millions of dollars)

COUNTRY	TELECOMMUNICATIONS SECTOR	ELECTRICITY SECTOR	
		GENERATION	DISTRIBUTION
Bolivia	610	250	200
Peru	n.a.	244	25.6

Source: Authors' compilation from the database of the research project.

In these and other countries, additional demands for expansion and improvements in the quality of services implicitly required large investments. Table IV-9 illustrates this in the case of telecommunications, in which investment commitments have helped to rapidly incorporate new technologies, provide new services and greatly increase access to basic telephone services.

In telecommunications, the investment commitments were actually exceeded, and the sector grew dynamically in all countries (see table IV-10). This is largely explained by the opening up of the sector to international investors and their struggle for regional market share, as well as the existing levels of pent-up demand.

---

31 In Bolivia's capitalization process, the State provided the State company, and the national or foreign investor contributed a level of capital equivalent to the market value of the State company, creating a company of double the value. The investor received 50% of the shares and took administrative control of the company, and the remainder of the shares were distributed to the citizens either directly or through the reformed pension fund system.

Table IV-9

INVESTMENT IN EXPANSION AND MODERNIZATION COMMITMENTS IN THE TELECOMMUNICATIONS SECTOR

COUNTRY	EXPANSION PROGRAMME (IN MILLIONS OF DOLLARS)	AMOUNT	YEARS	FULFILMENT RATE
Argentina	Telefónica +Telecom	15 000	1991-1997	more than 100%
Bolivia	Entel	408	1996-1998	more than 100%
	Other	300	1996-1997	
Mexico	Telmex	13 000	1990-1997	more than 100%
Peru	Telefónica del Perú	2009	1994-1997	more than 100%

Source: Authors' compilation from the database of the research project.

Table IV-10

INDICATORS OF SUPPLY, TECHNOLOGICAL PROGRESS AND PRODUCTIVITY IN TELECOMMUNICATIONS

	1986	1989	1990	1991	1992	1993	1994	1995	1996
TELEPHONE DENSITY (NUMBER OF LINES IN SERVICE PER 100 INHABITANTS)									
Argentina	6.7	n.a.	9.5	9.7	11.0	12.1	14.1	15.9	n.a.
Chile	6.6	7.4	8.9	9.0	9.9	11.4	12.1	13.6	14.3
Brazil	3.7	n.a.	5.7	6.0	6.4	6.8	7.3	7.4	n.a.
Costa Rica	6.9	n.a.	9.3	9.9	10.3	11.3	13.0	16.3	n.a.
Mexico	4.9	5.9	6.5	7.1	7.8	8.6	9.4	9.7	9.4
Peru	n.a.	n.a.	n.a.	n.a.	2.0	2.9	3.4	4.7	5.9
United States	41.4	n.a.	54.5	55.3	56.4	57.7	60.2	62.6	n.a.
DIGITALIZATION (PERCENTAGE)									
Argentina	0	0	0	12	32	54	72	85	96
Chile	37	51	64	70.6	76	100	100	100	100
Mexico	14	27	29	39	52	65	83	88	90
Peru	n.a.	n.a.	n.a.	n.a.	n.a.	53	77	85	88
Latin America	1.4	16.6	23.6	27.8	39.6	49.8	60.7	69	74.5
United States	26	41	47	52.7	58.7	66	74.1	78.4	80.5
LINES IN SERVICE PER EMPLOYEE									
Brazil	70	80	85	90	100	110	130	160	170
Chile	65	70	84	125	152	177	208	235	291
Argentina	70	59	62	70	90	110	150	170	296
Mexico	95	100	110	120	130	150	160	170	160
Peru	n.a.	n.a.	n.a.	n.a.	n.a.	n.a.	98	155	281
Uruguay	72	59	60	65	65	70	100	110	150
Latin America	72	78	86	98	110	123	139	158	185
United States	140	150	149	154	163	170	174	183	190

Source: Authors' compilation from the database of the research project.

c.   Pricing Incentives

In the regulated markets of some countries, the pricing model ensured a minimum return on the cost of the fixed assets required to expand the system, which served to spur new investments. As indicated above, this occurred in Bolivia, Chile and Peru, although some companies still made a much higher return than the minimum stipulated level. In the telecommunications sector in several countries, the pricing model was set at the time of privatization based on a high initial price which was indexed to inflation. This guaranteed significant benefits for the private owners, but it has prevented consumers from benefiting from productivity gains. In many cases, cross-subsidies between services were maintained for some time, phasing out gradually. Some countries established mechanisms to finance subsidies to low income groups who cannot pay the prices charged by the privatized company.[32]

The introduction of competition in these services forced countries to reform pricing legislation, incorporating new pricing models which will apply in the coming years. This process generates uncertainty in the private sector.

d.   Other Types of Incentives

Another way of providing incentives for private investment, specifically in the case of the electricity sector, has been for the State to guarantee energy purchases in generation, transmission or distribution projects.

The lack of incentives to encourage expansion in electricity generation in Colombia led the State to guarantee payment for the purchase of energy in projects to the value of US$ 3 billion. These investments have increased the capacity of the thermoelectric component in electricity supply, improving generating capacity and easing problems caused by hydrological factors.

In Mexico, private investment was geared towards projects to expand the electricity system managed by the State. Build-operate-transfer (BOT) contracts were drawn up in generation and transmission, as were contracts for the construction of complementary works, and independent production schemes were developed. From the outset, private sector participation in the electricity industry was seen as complementary. It has become increasingly important over the years, however, and in some activities it is now crucial. In 1997-2000 private companies are expected to finance 48% of all investment destined to expand the Sistema Eléctrico National (National Electricity System).

---

32 In the Colombian telecommunications sector, the Solidarity and Redistribution Fund was established to provide subsidies, which were partly financed by charging a higher prices to high income customers.

Brazil has lagged far behind in terms of investment levels, because of the fiscal constraints on investment by State-owned companies and a long period of transition during which uncertainty in the business environment was a disincentive for large-scale private investment.

e.   State Sponsored Investment

In most countries the State participated strongly in investment in electricity, using its own resources to invest in providing electricity to the whole population. The State played an important role in sectoral investment not only in countries like Mexico (where the electricity system is still State-run) and Brazil (which only opened up the sector to private investment in the late 1990) but also in other countries in which the private sector was participating. In Argentina, for example, the State continued to head up large investments in bi-national hydroelectric plants and the expansion of nuclear energy. The combined investment of the public and private sectors paved the way for an annual increase of 30% in installed generating capacity. The State also played an active role in distribution, carrying out electricity projects in areas with a lower population density. In Peru, of the total US$ 330 million of projected investment in generation over the next few years, 51% will be met by the State; the same will also occurs in transmission and distribution projects (table IV-11).

2.   Future Prospects

Reforms in the electricity and telecommunications sectors were designed to increase private sector investment. National and international investors reacted by channelling resources into those services and segments of the market that guaranteed the highest return. The outlook for these sectors depends on the following factors:

a)   The regulatory role of the State: Until now, the State has focused on creating incentives for the private sector and to a much lesser extent on defending consumer interests. While this has served to attract large conglomerates to infrastructure activities in the short term, competition will suffer in the medium term if a high degree of concentration prevails in these industries. Monopoly profits damage productive sectors as well as small consumers. Future development thus depends on strengthening the institutional framework (that is, regulation and supervising functions, and the legislation and rules that govern the markets).

b)   The convergence between private and social interests: Private companies only allocate their resources to profitable market segments. In no country are firms under any obligation to continue expanding the systems once the initial investment commitments have been carried out. This is not a

Table IV-11
INVESTMENT BEFORE AND AFTER PRIVATIZATIONS IN THE ELECTRICITY SECTOR

Country	Public sector (Annual average in millions of dollars)	Private sector (Annual average in millions of dollars)	Total electricity sector (Annual average in % of GDP)	Total electricity projections (Annual average in millions of dollars)	Projections of annual capacity increase	Projections of demand growth (Annual percentage)
Argentina	1970-1989: 1727 1993-1996: 700	1993-1996: Distribution: 284 Generation: 65		1998-2005: Private sector: 714 Public sector: 240	1998-2003: Period: 25% Annual: 4.5%	1992-1996: 7.0%
Bolivia		1996-1997: 84		1998-2002 Generation: 41.5 Distribution:51.5	1998-2002: Over 7 % With export prospects	1998-2002: 7 %
Brazil			1970-1980: 2.1 1981-1990: 1.5 1991-1992: 1.2 1993-1997: 0.6		1998-2000: 3.5 % Deficit risk: 1998: 15% 1999: 13%	1998-2000: 5.0 %
Colombia	1987-1990: 94 1991-1997: 101 1995-1997: 298	1991-1994: 15 1995-1997: 280	1980-1989: 2.8 1990-1995: 2.3 1996-1997: 2.5			
Chile	1973-1981: 302 1982-1988: 346 1989-1996: 280	1989-1996: 328	1980-1985: 1.8 1986-1989: 1.6 1990-1997: 1.5	1998-2000: 800 Investment in gas pipelines: 500	1997-2005: 9.3 %	1989-1998: 7.5% 1997-2000: 8.5%
Mexico	1989-1997: 1762	Contributes to financing: 1989-1995: 514		1997-2006: 25114 Public sector: 52% Private financing: 48%	1997-2006: Generation: 4.5 % Transmission: 2.5% Distribution: 1.9%	
Peru	1993-1997: 62	Investment in distribution: 1994-1997: 72	1970-1980: 3.2 1981-1990: 2.9 1991-1995: 0.7	Transmission and distribution of public + private sector 1997-2005: 114 Generation: (49% private, 51% public) In execution: 1996-2000: 127 Projected: 1997-2000: 330	Interconnected Southern System: 1997-2000: 9.9 % Interconnected Central-North System: 1997-2001: 10.4 %	1981-1990: 2.3 % 1991-1996: 4.4% Interconnected Southern System: 1997-2000: 9.9 % Interconnected Central-North System: 1997-2001: 7.7 %

Source: Authors' compilation from the database of the research project.

major problem in telecommunications, given that competition between operators at the global level and the speed of technological progress suggest that the sector will continue to grow for some time, but the story is different in the electricity sector. In the pre-reform period, the State carried out infrastructure development as a way of creating economies of scale and fostering growth. In the post-reform period investments are currently determined by profitability, together with low levels of risk and uncertainty. The State has to balance this against the demands of competitiveness and benefits for consumers. Indeed, given that the same international operators are present in different countries, a similar institutional framework should be established among them to keep the sector from falling behind in any country that chooses to implement change on its own. At the same time, the institutional framework should be strengthened to ensure greater competition.

c)   *How the least attractive markets are handled*: With a few exceptions, regulation has not determined either the targets or the means by which necessary investments can be carried out in markets that do not attract private interest. In the transitional period, the State has assumed this task, which raises the question of whether it should continue to do so in the future. Only in a few countries and certain market segments have incentives been developed to meet targets of providing broad-scale coverage. Private companies will not provide services in less profitable areas unless there is a scheme to establish both specific service targets and a clear, equitable mechanism for financing the necessary investments.

C. REFORM OF ROAD INFRASTRUCTURE

As in the case of the electricity and telecommunications sectors, private participation in road infrastructure was stimulated by the public sector in an effort to overcome the sharp deficit in investment resulting from the State financial crisis of the 1980s. One consequence of this lack of investment was that the highways deteriorated. With very few exceptions in the region, recent investments represent restoration projects or a timid step toward the reconstruction of lost competitiveness.

The implementation of large infrastructure projects under the new concession arrangements requires the joint participation of a number of actors –such as construction firms, financial institutions, institutional investors and governments– each if which has a different logic with regard to the profitability of the business. This type of undertaking was unknown in the region before the early 1990s. Consequently, more than a few problems arose in the course of the first efforts. For instance, many companies failed as a result of financial difficulties (this was the case in Mexico), and the construction firms lacked experience with the demands of completing the projects on time, with the type of financing involved, and with operating and administering the concessions.

The governments also faced unforeseen problems during the process, such as financial crises in the projects, the inability to fulfil the contracts, lack of supervision on the jobs, and lack of standards and rules. As a result, this process is still in transition, and any evaluation of the results to date will be far from conclusive. What can be analysed at the moment are the lessons learned from developments in the different countries, which have to do with the experience gained on the part of concessionaires, governments, financial institutions and users.

1. Reforms to the Institutional and Legal Framework

In order to spur private sector participation in road infrastructure, governments had to change or adapt the legislation and norms governing concessions, bidding, contracts and guarantees. Their efforts, which began in the early 1990s, were mainly directed at strengthening the legal basis which would give support and stability to the rules in the bidding and adjudication processes, as well as making sure the contracts were legally consistent. The degree of progress and achievements in consolidating the legal changes varied considerably among the different countries.

Some countries –Argentina, Chile and Mexico– sought to implement a broader reform of the State through constitutional and legislative reforms of a more far-reaching nature, and it was in this context that the concessions in road infrastructure were developed. In other countries –for example, Brazil– a legal framework was established which provided broad support for the privatization of State companies and concessions of public services. This occurred without thorough reforms to the State apparatus or to the regulatory framework. The changes undertaken in Colombia and Peru, in turn, focused much more on administrative reforms and the reorganization of the State apparatus itself (see table IV-12).

2. The Establishment of State Guarantees

Although there is no consensus on the benefits of offering State guarantees to spur private investment, half of the countries studied provided them. In these cases the underlying assumption is that the success of the concessions depends on risks being shared appropriately between the concessionaire and the State. The guarantees given to the concessionaires and their financial backers form part of this distribution of risks.

Table IV-12
REFORM OF THE STATE: LAWS ON ROAD CONCESSIONS

Argentina	Reform of State law: Changed the law on concessions for public works and permitted tolls Decree 1,817/92: Increased length of concession to 13 years
Brazil	Federal Law 8,666/93:Regulated bidding and contracting by public entities Federal Law 8,987/95 (and its complement 9,074/95): Regulated concessions for public services and contracts with private concessionaires Federal Law 9,277/96: Delegated to the State and municipalities the ability to grant road concessions
Chile	Decree 164, 1991: Regulated granting of concessions on all public works Supreme decree 240, 1991: Regulated concession and defined bidding process and concession contracts as result of negotiations with private sector
Colombia	Decree 2,171/92: Made Ministry of Public Works into Ministry of Transport and created Invias Law 60/93: Redefined competition of various levels of government, leaving road network to Invias Law 80/93 (General statute on administrative contracting): Defined concession contracts and obligations involved in maintaining economic and financial equilibrium of the contract Law 105/93 (Transport law): Introduced ability to give guarantees to concessionaires Law 99/93 (Environmental law): Established environmental licences Law 188/95: Consolidated road decentralization
Mexico	Promoted road concessions within a scheme to involve private firms in i nfrastructure investment
Peru	Decree Law 674/92: Confirmed intention to privatize State enterprises and attract foreign investment in road network Decree Law 758 (Private investment promotion law in infrastructure and public services): Enabled government to negotiate concession contracts with national and foreign legal persons Supreme decree 189/92: Regulated concessions on services in all levels of government and the toll levels Decree Law 839/96: Adjusted concession mechanism

Source: Authors' compilation from the database of the research project.

In Chile, Colombia and Peru, the public sector reduced the level of uncertainty facing private investors by guaranteeing profit levels, ensuring income based on minimum traffic levels or covering a certain percentage of the cost, or with other formulae.

In Colombia the so-called second generation projects, that is, those corresponding to a second wave of concessions, incorporated government guarantees which did not figure in the first projects and which were necessary in order to attract interest from the private sector. The State committed to assuming the cost of land expropriations required to carry out the projects, covering the risks associated with terrorist attacks and with changes in environmental laws and collecting the tolls in areas where the communities were opposed to the projects. In the case of Chile, from the outset the concession law introduced legal mechanisms which were designed to limit the risks that the concessionaires would assume during the stages of construction and operation or might face as a result of disputes with the State and changes in the tax regime (Moguillansky, 1997a). Judging by the statements of foreign investors in the local press, Chile's concession system is considered to entail low risk. Investors base this conclusion on the following factors: (a) Chile's good country risk rating; (b) the existence of a regulated system that clearly defines the rules of the game for participants; and (c) State guarantees for traffic flows, which make the Chilean system predictable and profitable over time, avoiding speculation over future benefits (see table IV-13).

Table IV-13

STATE GUARANTEES FOR ROAD INFRASTRUCTURE CONCESSIONS

Argentina	Concessions have no guarantee of minimum traffic flow or State guarantees
Brazil	Concessions have no guarantee of minimum traffic flow or State guarantees
Chile	Guarantee of minimum income (up to 70%), depending on level of risk involved in project
Colombia	Ability to grant guarantee to private concessionaires from national budget Possibility of delegating process of property acquisition Time limit on guarantee of minimum income through concept of expected income: once the expected income is reached, the concession reverts to the State
Mexico	Concessions have no guarantee of minimum traffic flow or State guarantees
Peru	Levels of monthly income are guaranteed by contract with the government

Source: Authors' compilation from the database of the research project.

D. THE EVOLUTION OF INVESTMENTS AND PRIVATE SECTOR PARTICIPATION

In the second half of the 1990s, large investments in road infrastructure took place in Chile, Mexico and Peru. Investments were more moderate in Argentina and Colombia, whereas in Brazil they remained below the levels seen in the previous two decades (table IV-14).

Private participation accounts for part of this dynamism, especially in Argentina, Chile, Colombia and Mexico. In Argentina private concessionaires invested an annual average of US$ 217 million in road construction between 1991 and 1997, equivalent to about 40% of total investments in the sector. In Chile investments reached an annual average of US$ 256 million between 1995 and 1997, when private investment began to materialize. Mexico is a special case because of the amount of resources spent (around US$ 2 billion a year between 1991 and 1994, which is practically double the amount invested by the public sector) and because of the scale of failure. In Colombia, the private sector invested a total of US$ 360 million between 1994 and 1997, which in 1997 represented about 42% of all the resources invested in road infrastructure.

Table IV-14
INVESTMENT IN ROAD INFRASTRUCTURE, 1971-1996
(Index numbers based on constant prices; period 1986-1990 = 100)

	ARGENTINA	BRAZIL a/	CHILE	COLOMBIA	MEXICO	PERU
1971/1975	177	144	n.a.	n.a.	133	265
1976/1980	220	155	n.a.	n.a.	127	257
1981/1985	114	79	107	n.a.	155	399
1986/1990	100	100	100	100b/	100	100e/
1991/1993	74	78	160	86c/	371	189f/
1994/1996	117	95	328	129d/	334	453

Source: Authors' compilation from the database of the research project.
a/ Estimates, on the basis that road infrastructure matched the rate of growth of local transport.
b/ 1987-1990.
c/ 1991-1992.
d/ 1993-1995.
e/ Includes 1991.
f/ Excludes 1991.

In Argentina, Chile and Mexico, private capital accounted for between 20% and 70% of total investment (see table IV-15), whereas the share in Brazil and Peru remains very low. These two countries have only recently initiated the process, with the aim of maintaining and modernizing the roads with the highest level of traffic density.

Table IV-15
SHARE OF PRIVATE CAPITAL IN ROAD INFRASTRUCTURE INVESTMENT, 1991-1997
(percent)

	ARGENTINA	CHILE	MEXICO
1991-1993	46.4	0.0	69.8
1994	55.0	0.0	58.6
1995	35.5	7.6	27.2
1996	29.2	22.3	12.1
1997	n.a.	40.9	n.a.

Source: Authors' compilation from the database of the research project.

1. The Response of the Concessionaires

The consortiums were generally led by domestic construction companies that were accustomed to carrying out public works projects. For these companies, the concessions represented an opportunity to use their spare capacity and receive income for construction, repair and improvement services they provided directly to the concessionaire. They were thus able to avoid the delays and uncertainties that they encountered with government payments. In some countries, foreign consortiums were encouraged to participate so as to increase the levels of experience and competition in the bidding process, which the country lacked.

The concessionaires transformed –to varying degrees– the approach of public works construction companies by adopting the role of service providers. The notion of risk was also introduced in investments in roads, as was the need to negotiate with the authorities to obtain some level of guarantee against market uncertainties.

The financial backers of the concessionaires had the opportunity to place their resources at relatively high rates of return, initially in the short term (the construction stage) and afterwards in the long term (during the term of the concession). This was justified by the uncertainty of this new line of business.

2. The Response of the Government

Road concessions provided a series of benefits for governments which allowed them to allocate available resources to other types of expenditure and to carry out infrastructure works which would otherwise have been postponed. Indeed, governments avoided the costs of maintaining and improving the stretch of roads that were operated in concession. Because of their volume of traffic, these roads had suffered the most damage. This helped to recover the value of the national patrimony and to gain additional benefits over the concession period. However, the entire portfolio of projects that can be put to concession (i.e., with sufficient traffic to make the business profitable) is relatively small in relation to the countries' total road infrastructure requirements. This means that the State will have to maintain and repair the existing network, leading it to the search for new formulae and alternative sources of sustainable finance in the long term.

3. Financing the Concessions

The programme of public infrastructure concessions posed a challenge for the construction industry, as well as for the domestic financial system, which until then had not dealt with this type of business. Three types of domestic financial institutions can participate in this process: (a) private investment companies; (b) domestic and foreign banks; and (c) institutional investors (pension funds, insurance companies and investment funds).

Several private investment companies joined construction companies to form consortiums, which participated in the bidding for infrastructure projects. An analysis of the process in Chile shows that at the beginning, they contributed only a small share of their own resources for the financing, which made it difficult for the commercial banks to approve the projects. In the concessions carried out after 1997, the consortiums substantially raised their financing levels by contributing more of their own resources, which also helped to incorporate foreign banks in the construction phase of the project. In Colombia and Brazil foreign banks also provided capital for the operations phase of the concession.

The other main source of financing was the domestic banking system. For banks to participate, legislative guarantees and a greater contribution of the concessionaires' own resources were required. In some countries domestic banks have thus far only given short-term loans with relatively high costs in terms of interest rates and commissions. These loans have to be refinanced by the consortium once the construction phase is finished; otherwise their financial costs will rise considerably, affecting the profitability of the project (see table IV-16).

Table IV-16
TYPES OF CONCESSION FINANCING IN ROAD INFRASTRUCTURE

COUNTRY	CHARACTERISTICS OF FINANCING
Argentina	No consolidated road financing scheme to date Few important concession projects without State support Private financing from Argentine banks
Brazil	Long-term financing for concessionaires provided exclusively by the National Bank for Economic and Social Development (BNDES) Bridge loans from foreign banks, awaiting long-term foreign financing
Chile	For construction: Chilean and foreign commercial banks For long-term refinancing: insurance companies, national investment funds and AFPs (these have yet to materialize)
Colombia	Financing for construction from Colombian financial entities and, for some projects, from foreign bank affiliates
Mexico	Resources from governmental units (such as Capufe, Pemex and state governments), up to 30% Project costs and right of way charged to national budget Private financing from Mexican and foreign banks

Source: Authors' compilation from the database of the research project.

The institutions which theoretically should participate in the long-term financing of concession projects –but which so far have failed to do so– are the private pension funds. In countries in which pension funds have been established, their participation could take a number of forms:
a) acquiring quotas issued by other investment funds, which in turn acquire bonds or shares in the concessionaire;
b) acquiring bonds or other instruments issued directly by the concessionaire and placed through a public offering (these bonds could correspond to the construction phase or to the operating period of the concession); and
c) acquiring a stake in the concessionaire once the period of concession has begun.

In Chile, the ministers of Public Works and of Finance have made great efforts to get institutional investors to participate in financing infrastructure projects. Apparently, this participation will be secured through infrastructure bond issues, the design of which took into account the form and transferability of the instruments, interest rates and flexibility, interest payments and amortization, and the terms of guarantees. Other factors considered include clauses addressing rescue, representation and payment currency; the declaration and security of the issuer; its obligations, limitations and restrictions; and its risk rating. The bonds would cover the construction and operation phases of the concession, and the instrument would carry a sovereign guarantee on 100% of the value of the debt.

4. Future Prospects

Private concessions will never fully substitute for public investment in roads. The stretches of road that are profitable for the private sector constitute a small fraction of the whole road network, although they involve a large amount of resources that will be invested in the coming years. Nevertheless, governments must address and overcome several problems to ensure the success of the process.

a) As of 1998, no country had established institutions or mechanisms to regulate the concessions. The lack of regulation has had several negative effects, such as shortcomings in technical information and engineering projects; the possibility of changes in the route and the recurrent imposition of additional works; inadequate or superficial cost estimations, which have an unfavourable bearing on the price of the tolls and consequently on the competitiveness of the system.

b) The authorities have lacked technical capacity in the auction and bidding processes, and the interests of consumers have been sidelined.

c) The concession programmes have often been characterized by contradictions between the objective of maximizing the fiscal revenue from the award of the concession and that of maximizing investment commitments in the auctions and bidding processes. When the government's main concern was to secure a windfall, the investment commitments were relaxed.

d) The resistance of local communities to paying tolls and, in some cases, land improvement taxes hinder the concession process. Problems between users and service providers are exacerbated when there is a lack of regulatory mechanisms or recourse to dispute arbitration.

e) Tolls have frequently been set too high, which has in some cases offset the reduction in operational costs –stemming from higher security, less damage to vehicles and the faster journey time– obtained by the repair and improvement of the stretches of road awarded in concession.

CHAPTER V

SYNTHESIS AND CONCLUSIONS

This book has presented an analysis of capital accumulation in Latin America over the last decade. Although it only studied eight countries, together they account for 80% of the population and almost 90% of regional output. The analytical focus considered macroeconomic, sectoral and microeconomic factors, together with their effects on capital formation. This methodology enabled us to assess the impact of structural transformation, institutional change, market structure and firms' strategies with regard to investment decisions. Sectoral analysis made it possible to identify resource allocation after the reforms and the strengths and weaknesses generated as a result.

A. THE POST-REFORM TRANSITION STAGE AND ITS EFFECTS ON INVESTOR BEHAVIOUR

As discussed above, the countries are still experiencing a transition stage in which the economic reforms have led to a series of reactions in the area of investment decisions, which affect both the short and medium term but which will not necessarily continue in the long term. These reactions are related to the existence of two types of investment determinants: permanent and transitory. The latter had a very strong influence on investment in the 1990s.

Permanent factors are those which have always determined investment in market economies. They include fluctuations in demand, the macroeconomic environment, relative prices, technological progress and the market positioning strategies of firms. Transitory factors are those which are only important in the short and medium term following the implementation

141

of the reforms. They have worked alongside permanent factors throughout the transition stage. Chile is the only country that managed to conclude the major part of the transition stage in the 1990s, achieving a reasonably consolidated model.

All the countries experienced two phases in the transition process, characterized by different performance, as described in detail in the first chapter. During the first phase most countries experienced a negative macroeconomic environment for investment, and the transitory reactions of firms tended to depress investment levels even further. Key among the reactions were the extreme caution demonstrated by firms and their efforts to rationalize productive processes. During the second phase the opposite occurred: investment was boosted by improved macroeconomic conditions, and the transitory reactions of firms now tended to increase investment. There was a strong and generalized push to modernize machinery (in contrast to the "disembodied" technological progress that characterized the rationalization phase), which aimed to reduce costs and improve quality (rather than expand capacity).

Transitory reactions also occurred within sectors. In the second transitory phase, all cases saw a short wave of investment based on one-time opportunities, which ended automatically as soon as the opportunities were exhausted. Important examples include the strategic repositioning of transnational firms in Latin America, as a result of their liquidity and ability to change their market position in the wake of institutional reform; large investments by privatized firms, which were conditions of the contracts negotiated during the bidding process and which took the form of investment commitments, expansion and modernization; and the particularly high levels of investment in telecommunications that began once the private sector became involved. These and other elements discussed in the sectoral chapters of the book generated far higher investment levels than in "normal" times.

Indeed, during the second phase of post-reform investment, some countries managed to raise average investment levels above those recorded prior to the crisis in the 1980s. In the two largest countries (Brazil and Mexico), however, investment remained below that registered in the 1970s and 1960s. Chile is the only country where the reforms reached a degree of maturity in the 1990s: the transitory factors were coming to an end and thus had a much weaker influence on investment. In the first half of the 1980s a massive private investment drive took off in Chile, fostered by State policies to manage the macroeconomy efficiently and to guarantee high profitability and low levels of uncertainty. By the late 1990s, this investment growth was tailing off owing to the falling returns to natural resource investment and the fall-out from the Asian crisis (Moguillansky, 1999).

B. AN OVERALL CONCLUSION: AN UNCERTAIN FUTURE FOR AGGREGATE INVESTMENT

Firms are now confronted by two new situations: macroeconomic instability owing to the volatility of foreign capital flows, and the consolidation of the new institutional framework brought about by the reforms. These generate a new set of microeconomic incentives, but there is no guarantee that they will resolve the equation of profitability and risk in a way that will increase investment in capacity expansion beyond what the previous economic model achieved.

Once the transition phase is complete and the incentives stemming from deregulation and market opening are no longer so strong, the region will be confronted by an unstable picture:

a) *High levels of vulnerability:* This is a consequence of financial globalization, the lack of a global and regional architecture to protect economies from the volatility of international capital flows and the fragility of the region's financial systems. These factors do not provide a positive macroeconomic environment for investment in capacity expansion, given that this type of investment involves considerable sunk costs.

b) *Lower profits and higher risks:* These stem from changes in the behaviour of domestic firms in tradable goods sectors. Before the onset of macroeconomic instability caused by the debt crisis in the 1980s, investment in tradable goods was very profitable –although this profitability was often rather skewed owing to high protection levels– thanks to a microeconomic environment of low risk and uncertainty, and a cost of capital which in many countries was negative. The economic reforms, in contrast, created a microeconomic environment characterized by an open, unprotected market with higher risks and greater uncertainties. For this reason national firms have concentrated investment in highly profitable sectors, unwilling to take the risk of developing projects that require innovation, research and development, that have a long lead time, that are exposed to low profit margins or that reap benefits only in the long term.

c) *Lower public investment in infrastructure:* Before the crisis in the public sector, governments invested in public utilities with a view to creating positive externalities but generally without considering whether the projects would be profitable, risky or uncertain. Privatization of these sectors brought about demands for higher profits, the incorporation of risk into pricing decisions, and an aversion to macro- and microeconomic uncertainty. If the State does not compensate for these risks, particularly in energy sectors (electricity and hydrocarbons), road infrastructure, water and sanitation, there is no reason to expect that investment should be any higher than in the past.

d) *New firms and business strategies:* Throughout the 1970s and 1980s, foreign direct investment (FDI) flooded out of the region, but the 1990s witnessed an increase in FDI, particularly as a result of mergers and acquisitions of local firms by transnational corporations. Macroeconomic stability, market liberalization and deregulation in Latin America attracted capital inflows. The question is whether this will bring about a new investment cycle, with capital going to new sectors and businesses. To date there have been no clear signs about whether this will occur, which makes it difficult to forecast future investment. While this seems to be the most positive way to increase investment, it will also increase competition for national firms.

In sum, the new environment created by the reforms combines macroeconomic uncertainty, stemming from the globalization of financial markets, with microeconomic uncertainties, related to the behaviour of firms in light of the new rules of the game prevailing in the market. These two types of uncertainty reinforce each other, affecting the "entrepreneurial spirit" and propensity to invest.

C. SECTORAL BEHAVIOUR AND WEAKNESSES

Thus far, post-reform investment performance has not been sufficient to provide high and sustained levels of growth, and many countries experienced extremely volatile growth rates in the 1990s. Furthermore, at the sectoral level, investment was not just low, but its composition actually reduced countries' capacity for successful insertion into the world economy in the future. Few countries saw investment grow in tradables sectors. What little investment did occur in tradables flowed into primary export sectors, which suffer from high levels of price volatility and consequent economic vulnerability. Low investment in manufacturing explains the loss of the sector's importance in total GDP and the deterioration of the sector's trade balance, with the sole exception of Mexico.

These results merit comment. First, as shown above, the period analysed represents a transition stage in which the economy slowly adapts to a new investment regime. Second, in the 1990s investment performance was affected by macroeconomic fluctuations. The instability in the wake of the 1994 Mexican crisis, the Asian crisis and the Russian financial crisis, as well as the macroeconomic response to these external shocks, changed the way in which resources were allocated. This was particularly evident in countries where the reforms had sought to serve two rather contradictory objectives, in which liberalization was used both to stabilize prices and to change resource allocation.

In this light, the conclusions of this study point to the need for a revision of the reforms. We are not advocating a deepening of liberalization as extreme liberals espouse, nor a return to closed, State-run economies as the severest critics of the reforms would have. Rather, any revision of the reforms should seek to strengthen the complementary roles of the State and the private sector to foster investment growth and more efficient resource allocation over the long term.

1. Industrial Sector

Except in Chile, industrial investment was for the most part defensive. The coefficient of sectoral investment was lower in the 1990s than the average rates during the 1970s and 1980s. In addition, the allocation of investment was heterogeneous –with strong investment growth concentrated in branches that produced industrial commodities based on natural resources– which added to the growing disarticulation and disintegration of production chains.

Concentration in natural resource–based manufacturing essentially removed the region from the high growth, high technology sectors that dominate international trade. The only exceptions were areas that benefited from specific sectoral policy, such as the automotive industries in Argentina, Brazil and Mexico and electronic assembly plants in Brazil and Mexico.

At the same time, there was an increasing disarticulation, or even disintegration, of production chains, since the fast-growing sectors did not transmit their dynamism to other parts of the economy. The result was increased the reliance on imported inputs and the strengthening of assembly operations. Thus, a key weakness of the post-reform model was its inability to increase demand for productive, high-skilled employment or to support sectors that would increase local technological capacity. The resulting need to import factor inputs led to a deterioration in the balance of payments.

a. The Manufacturing Trade Balance Followed a Negative Trend

As the post-reform period progressed, the trade balance deteriorated sharply in the sectors in which investment grew fastest, and also in the manufacturing sector as a whole. The deficit reached and in some cases surpassed that of the pre-reform period. This happened both in the most industrialized countries (Argentina, Brazil and Colombia) and in Chile and Peru. The rising trade deficit is significant because it demonstrates that even in countries with a growing proportion of new investment in export activities, the productive structure –particularly for assembly plants– requires higher import levels. The external balance tends to be achieved at times of recession or macroeconomic adjustment, rather than, as was expected, at times of growth.

Manufacturing export growth was evident in Chile through the mid-1990s and in Mexico, particularly after the tequila crisis. Chile continues to maintain an export orientation, and a high degree of diversity in its markets, while the Mexican manufacturing sector is dominated by assembly plants that sell the majority of their output to the United States. Argentina occupies an intermediate position; its exports are largely sold in Mercosur. Manufacturing in Brazil and Colombia, however, continues to be focused largely on serving the domestic market.

Although export growth was strongly linked with investment in some countries, branches that received relatively low investment levels also began to export. Nonetheless, the strong capital inflows and the resulting appreciation of local currencies made it impossible for exporters to maintain profits at a level that would enable an expansion of productive capacity. The result was a reduction in investment.

b. *The Bulk of Investment Was Concentrated in Transnational Corporations and National Conglomerates*

Transnational corporations have been keen to acquire firms with a high local and international market profile. This is evident not only in industry but also in other productive and public services sectors, which underwent privatization. Large firms in general benefited from the opening of trade and financial and capital markets, as well as from privatization. They implemented projects that were designed to modernize production and raise competitiveness, and they expanded productive capacity so that they could gain competitive advantage in fast-growing sectors. In the late 1990s, however, transnational companies began to buy up the highest profile firms from local groups.

c. *Small and Medium-sized Firms Were the Weakest Players in the Investment Process*

The available data on these firms in some countries indicate –particularly in the case of small firms– that they had only a marginal share in capital formation, which made them extremely vulnerable. Although growth and indirect demand from other fast-growing sectors enabled them to begin modernization, their development was constrained by a number of factors:
- The inability to compete with imported products, which appeared in all branches of manufacturing;
- The abolition of preferential loan rates and consequent reliance on the domestic financial system (which had prohibitively high rates), together with the firms' strong sensitivity to cyclical monetary adjustment; and

-   The end of technological development policies and technical assistance, although some countries maintained some of these support mechanisms.

2. *Mining and Hydrocarbon Sectors*

Institutional change in the mining and hydrocarbon sector expanded in the 1990s, to the extent that some countries actually privatized their deposits completely. Nonetheless, the economic power of these firms and the strategic nature of the product –particularly oil, on which the global competitiveness of the economy depends– have forced the countries to carry out privatization very carefully, in some cases establishing strategic partnerships with transnational capital instead of privatizing.

a. *The Primary Objective of the Sectoral Reforms Was to Encourage Investment by Domestic and Foreign Private Firms*

Institutional change deregulated the treatment of foreign investment and modified the administrative regimes governing mining concessions and oil legislation. It simplified the tax regime for mining and hydrocarbons, and it strengthened the property rights of large firms in these sectors. By doing this, governments aimed to attract new actors to the sector and to compensate for the fall in public investment caused by fiscal constraints.

b. *Firm Strategies Fostered Investment Growth*

Both State firms and transnational corporations experienced investment growth. Aiming to increase their share of the world market, State firms implemented groundbreaking policies: they formed strategic partnerships with transnational firms, internationalized production and invested heavily. Brazil and Mexico, however, did not form such partnerships. In the case of Brazil, the transformation process began only recently, and in the case of Mexico, the constitution bans the involvement of the private sector, even through strategic partnerships.

Chile benefited most from the increase in exploration and exploitation of mineral deposits in the 1990s. Its pioneering sectoral reforms attracted transnational mining companies just at a point when the global economy entered an upswing. This cycle began in the second half of the 1980s and was aided by the sharp increase in international prices, particularly of gold and copper, and by technological progress that enabled the industry to cut costs considerably. Mining investment in the 1990s accounted for four percentage points of the increase in investment as a share of GDP. The lack of a mining policy, however, prevented the sector's growth from having positive externalities on related sectors, such as machinery and equipment manufacturers and engineering, research and development activities into the diversification of copper usage. It also prevented the production of higher value added derivatives and the development of links to the domestic capital market.

As a share of GDP, mining investment grew fastest in Chile, followed by Peru and Argentina, while Brazil experienced zero growth. There are three principal reasons for this: institutional changes, which opened up new opportunities for investment in the first two countries; developments in the international market, which was positive for high-value minerals; and strong international liquidity, which enabled firms to tap large investment flows.

Given that quite a long time elapses between the discovery of reserves and exploitation, investment in Peru and Argentina was constrained by the sharp fall in mineral prices and illiquidity that followed the Asian and Russian crises. The Brazilian mining industry developed rather differently than that in other countries, principally because sectoral reform is quite recent and the main State firm, which was privatized in 1997, prioritized productivity increases over expanded production. The low level of investment relative to exploitation potential is also explained by the oversupply of Brazilian minerals in world markets, the lack of exploration and information on the country's reserves, and the high infrastructure costs in the Amazon region.

In the hydrocarbon sector, the participation of foreign investment either in stand-alone projects or in partnership with State firms heralds renewed growth. Foreign investment in the hydrocarbon industry has been incorporated into the different links of the production chain. On the one hand, changes in contracts encouraged exploration. On the other, a network of oil and gas pipelines developed as a result of private capital and government efforts to foster regional energy integration. In addition, partnerships between State firms and transnational corporations led to new exploitation projects both at home and abroad.

When discussing incentives for foreign investment, it is important to consider the other side of the coin, that is, the loss of income to the State and society as a whole, which stems from reductions in income tax and royalties. At the same time, the lack of incentives to encourage linkages between the extractive sectors and related manufacturing and services sectors has prevented the spread of technology and sharing of growth which these investments could generate.

3.   Infrastructure Sectors

Post-reform investment in infrastructure grew strongly in the 1990s relative to the 1980s –apart from in Brazil and Peru– and its share of GDP also increased.

a. The Telecommunications Sector Has Undoubtedly Been the Leader in this Process

Although most countries granted periods of monopoly rights to private firms, placing barriers to entry in these markets, five basic factors stimulated investment in the sector.
- The fight among the main transnational operators for market share at the global level was a major factor behind the investment effort of private monopolies in the region.
- The rapid technological development of the sector forced private monopolies to remain on the forefront of new technology in services, equipment and products so as not to lose their market share once the sector was liberalized.
- Pricing legislation provided high profits negotiated between the government and firms at the time of privatization.
- Large pent-up demand and technical deficiencies provided a tremendous opportunity in these markets for most large operators.
- The goals of expansion and high-quality service imposed during the privatization negotiations required large investments.

The main constraints on the future development of the telecommunications sector are the institutional weakness of regulators and poor competition policies. These failings slow pricing negotiations and the possibility of transferring some of the monopoly rents and productivity gains to consumers. In some countries, these weaknesses were highlighted when the opening of some market segments to competition was delayed, despite the fact that it was economically and technically feasible. In other countries, such as Chile in 1995, these failings led to a lack of legal instruments to block mergers and strategic partnerships between large firms, which undermined fair competition. The larger countries have expressed concern that the opportunity to develop domestic production would be lost; this is particularly the case in Brazil, which has the capacity to produce software and equipment.

b. Investment Growth is Least Widespread in the Electricity Sector

An objective assessment of investment performance in the electricity sector must take into account a number of key elements in order to avoid reaching erroneous conclusions about the process. These are as follows: (i) the situation prevailing in the sector before privatization and the requirements of the system's expansion; (ii) State participation in the sector, which varied among the countries; (iii) pricing legislation; and (iv) incentives for new firms to satisfy growing demand. Bearing these elements in mind, we conclude the following:
- The electricity sector experienced much less dynamic growth than did telecommunications, in both technological development and investment.

-   To date, it is only in Chile and Argentina that the private sector has worked to foster capital accumulation in the sector, but the quality of service has deteriorated.
-   Among the other countries, private investment grew thanks to specific sectoral policy instruments, such as purchase guarantees in Colombia and Mexico and capitalization or investment commitments in Bolivia and Peru. In Brazil, where privatization is still underway, the volume of both private and public investment has been quite low.
-   It is not certain that future private participation will meet the requirements to increase coverage. This is an important issue for governments and regulatory bodies. The future of the sector will depend on the strengthening of regulation, the creation of incentives and State action in areas in which providing service is not profitable for the private sector.

As in the case of telecommunications, weak institutions and regulations impede adequate electricity coverage and quality. The extreme case is Chile: a decade after the entire system was privatized, frequent power cuts in recent years demonstrated that while the post-reform rules of the game might have stimulated investment, but they did not ensure the quality or efficiency expected.

c.   *In the 1990s the Private Sector Became Involved in the Financing and Management of Road Infrastructure*

Road infrastructure concessions provided several benefits for governments, most importantly by freeing up resources for other types of spending. The private sector, for its part, benefited from the creation of a new business, which was complemented by financial, construction and management activities. Although private sector involvement means that the State does not have to bear the costs of maintaining and expanding heavily used roads, it is important to remember that the portfolio of projects for which concessions are possible is very small relative to the countries' total road infrastructure requirements.

Infrastructure concessions brought with them a new challenge not only for the construction industry, which had to incorporate new standards and modernize works, machinery and equipment, but also for the domestic financial system, which in the future will have to provide long-term instruments for refinancing during the operating stage of the projects.

As in the other infrastructure sectors that have been opened up to the private sector, one of the challenges to the efficient functioning of the concession programmes in the future is the creation of regulatory bodies and mechanisms. To date the lack of regulation has caused a number of problems in the sector, including poor quality technical information and engineering projects, and inadequate and superficial cost estimates. These problems have a negative effect on tolls and, consequently, on the competitiveness of the system.

BIBLIOGRAPHY

Abugattás, Luis (1999), "Estabilización macroeconómica, reforma estructural y comportamiento industrial: la experiencia peruana", Reformas económicas series, No. 48 (LC/L.1293), Santiago, Chile, Economic Commission for Latin America and the Caribbean (ECLAC).

Ayala Sánchez, Víctor H. (1998), "Impacto de las reformas estructurales globales y sectoriales sobre la inversión y productividad del sector hidrocarburos en Bolivia", Santiago, Chile, Economic Commission for Latin America and the Caribbean (ECLAC), unpublished.

Bacha, L.E. (ed.) (1993), *Saving and Investment Requirements for the Resumption of Growth in Latin America*, Washington, D.C., Inter-American Development Bank (IDB).

Barja Daza, Gover (1999a), "Las reformas estructurales bolivianas y su impacto sobre inversiones", Reformas económicas series, No.42 (LC/L.1287), Santiago, Chile, Economic Commission for Latin America and the Caribbean (ECLAC).

_____(1999b), "Inversión y productividad en la industria boliviana de telecomunicaciones", Reformas económicas series, No. 16 (LC/L.1173), Santiago, Chile, Economic Commission for Latin America and the Caribbean (ECLAC).

_____(1999c), "Inversión y productividad en la industria boliviana de la electricidad", Reformas económicas series, No. 15 (LC/L.1172), Santiago, Chile, Economic Commission for Latin America and the Caribbean (ECLAC).

Bielschowsky, Ricardo (1999a), "Investimentos na indústria brasileira depois da abertura e do real: o mini-ciclo de modernizações", Reformas económicas series, No. 44 (LC/L.1289), Santiago, Chile, Economic Commission for Latin America and the Caribbean (ECLAC).

————(1999b), "O setor elétrico no Brasil: investimentos deprimidos numa transição problemática", Brasilia, Economic Commission for Latin America and the Caribbean (ECLAC), unpublished.

Bisang, Roberto (1998), "Apertura, reestructuración industrial y conglomerados económicos", *Grandes empresas y grupos industriales latinoamericanos: expansión y desafíos en la era de la apertura y la globalización*, Wilson Peres Núñez (ed.), Mexico City, Siglo Veintiuno Editores.

Bisang, Roberto and Georgina Gómez (1999), "Las inversiones en la industria argentina en la década de los noventa", Reformas económicas series, No. 41 (LC/L.1286), Santiago, Chile, Economic Commission for Latin America and the Caribbean (ECLAC).

Bitrán, Daniel (1999), "México: inversiones en el sector de agua, alcantarillado y saneamiento", Reformas económicas series, No. 21 (LC/L.1197), Santiago, Chile, Economic Commission for Latin America and the Caribbean (ECLAC).

Caballero, R.J. and Robert S. Pindyck (1996), "Uncertainty, investment, and industry evolution", *International Economic Review*, vol. 37, No. 3.

Calderón Hoffmann, Alvaro and others (1995), "Mexico's incorporation into the new industrial order: foreign investment as a source of international competitiveness", Desarrollo productivo series, No. 21 (LC/G.1864), Santiago, Chile, Economic Commission for Latin America and the Caribbean (ECLAC).

Campodónico Sánchez, Humberto (1999a), "Las reformas estructurales del sector eléctrico peruano y las características de la inversión, 1992-2000", Reformas económicas series, No. 25 (LC/L.1209), Santiago, Chile, Economic Commission for Latin America and the Caribbean (ECLAC).

————(1999b), "Las reformas estructurales en el sector minero peruano y las características de la inversión 1992-2008", Reformas económicas series, No. 24 (LC/L.1209), Santiago, Chile, Economic Commission for Latin America and the Caribbean (ECLAC).

————(1999c), "La inversión en el sector petrolero peruano en el periodo 1993-2000", Reformas eonómicas series, No. 23 (LC/L.1207), Santiago, Chile, Economic Commission for Latin America and the Caribbean (ECLAC).

————(1999d), "La inversión en el sector de telecomunicaciones del Perú en el período 1994-2000", Reformas económicas series, No. 22 (LC/L.1206), Santiago, Chile, Economic Commission for Latin America and the Caribbean (ECLAC).

————(1996a), "Cambios en el régimen de contratación petrolera en América Latina en la década de los noventa" (LC/R.1626), Santiago, Chile, Economic Commission for Latin America and the Caribbean (ECLAC).

————(1996b), *El ajuste petrolero: políticas empresariales en América Latina de cara al 2000*, Lima, DESCO.

Cardoso, Eliana (1993), "Macroeconomic enviroment and capital formation in Latin America", *Striving for Growth after Adjustment: The Role of Capital*

Formation, Luis Servén and Andrés Solimano (eds.), Washington, D.C., World Bank.

Celani, Marcelo (1998), "Determinantes de la inversión en telecomunicaciones en Argentina", Reformas económicas series, No. 9 (LC/L.1157), Santiago, Chile, Economic Commission for Latin America and the Caribbean (ECLAC).

Chisari, Omar and Martín Rodríguez (1998), "Algunos determinantes de la inversión en sectores de infraestructura en la Argentina", Reformas económicas series, No. 8 (LC/L.1155), Santiago, Chile, Economic Commission for Latin America and the Caribbean (ECLAC).

Chudnovsky, Daniel and others (1995), "Más allá del flujo de caja: el boom de la inversión extranjera directa en la Argentina", *Desarrollo económico*, vol. 35, No. 137.

COCHILCO (Comision Chilena del Cobre), *Inversión extranjera en la minería chilena*, Santiago, Chile, various issues.

CODELCO-Chile (Corporación Nacional del Cobre de Chile) (1997), *Memoria anual*, Santiago, Chile.

CODELCO-Chile/SERNAGEOMIN (Corporación Nacional del Cobre de Chile and Servicio Nacional de Geología y Minería) (1997), *Direcmin: directorio minero de Chile, 1997*, Santiago, Chile.

Cominetti, Rossella (1996), "La privatización y el marco regulatorio en Bolivia y Nicaragua: un análisis comparativo", Reformas de política pública series, No. 43 (LC/L.973; LC/L.973/Add.1), Santiago, Chile, Economic Commission for Latin America and the Caribbean (ECLAC).

Corbo, Vittoria and Patricio Rojas Ramos (1993), "Investment, macroeconomic stability and growth: the Latin American experience", *Revista de análisis económico*, vol. 8, No. 1, Santiago, Chile, Instituto Latinoamericano de Doctrinas y Estudios Sociales (ILADES)/Universidad de Georgetown.

Cordero, José Antonio (1999), "El crecimiento económico y la inversión: el caso de Costa Rica", Reformas económicas series, No. 51 (LC/L.1346), Santiago, Chile, Economic Commission for Latin America and the Caribbean (ECLAC).

Damil, Mario and Roberto Frenkel (1987), "De la apertura a la crisis financiera: un análisis de la experiencia argentina de 1977-1982", *Ensayos económicos*, No. 37, Buenos Aires, Argentina.

De Moori Koening, María Virginia (1999), "Reformas económicas y la inversión en el sector minero argentino", Reformas económicas series, No. 50 (LC/L.1327), Santiago, Chile, Economic Commission for Latin America and the Caribbean (ECLAC).

Delgado, Ricardo (1998), "Inversiones en infraestructura vial: la experiencia argentina", Reformas económicas series, No. 6 (LC/L.1149), Santiago, Chile, Economic Commission for Latin America and the Caribbean (ECLAC).

Dixit, A. (1989), "Entry and exit decisions under uncertainty", *Journal of Political Economy*, vol. 97, No. 3.

ECLAC (Economic Commission for Latin America and the Caribbean), (1990-1999), *Economic Survey of Latin America and the Caribbean*, Santiago, Chile, various issues.

――――(1999), *Latin America and the Caribbean in the World Economy, 1998* (LC/G.2038-P), Santiago, Chile, March. United Nations publication, Sales No. E.99.II.G.3.

――――(1996), *Strengthening development: the interplay of macro- and microeconomics*, Libros de la CEPAL series, No. 42 (LC/G.1898/Rev.1-P), Santiago, Chile, March. United Nations publication, Sales No. E.96.II.G.2.

――――(1992), *Social equity and changing production patterns: an integrated approach*, Libros de la CEPAL series, No. 32 (LC/G.1701/Rev.1-P), Santiago, Chile, April. United Nations publication, Sales No. 92.II.G.5.

――――*Statistical Yearbook for Latin America and the Caribbean*, Santiago, Chile, various issues.

Edwards, Sebastián (1995), *Crisis and Reform in Latin America: From Despair to Hope*, New York, Oxford University Press.

Escobar de Médicigo, Rebeca (1999), "El cambio estructural de las telecomunicaciones y la inversión: el caso de México", Reformas económicas series, No. 17 (LC/L.1174), Santiago, Chile, Economic Commission for Latin America and the Caribbean (ECLAC).

Fainboim Yaker, Israel and Carlos Jorge Rodríguez Restrepo (1999), "El desarrollo de la infraestructura en Colombia en la década de los noventa", Reformas económicas series, No. 52 (LC/L.1348), Santiago, Chile, Economic Commission for Latin America and the Caribbean (ECLAC).

Fernández-Arias, Eduardo and Peter J. Montiel (1998), "Reform and growth in Latin America: All pain, no gain?", OCE Working Paper, No. 351, Washington, D.C., Inter-American Development Bank (IDB).

Ffrench-Davis, Ricardo and Stephany Griffith-Jones (eds.), (1995) *Coping with Capital Surges. The Return of Finance to Latin America*, Lynne Rienner Publishers, Boulder, CO.

Ffrench-Davis, Ricardo and Helmut Reisen (eds.) (1998), *Capital Flows and Investment Performance: Lessons from Latin America*, OECD Development Centre/ECLAC, Paris.

Frenkel, Roberto (1982), "Mercado financiero, expectativas cambiarias y movimientos de capital", *Desarrollo económico*, vol. 22, No. 87.

Gadano, Nicolás (1998), "Determinantes de la inversión en el sector petróleo y gas de la Argentina", Reformas económicas series, No. 7 (LC/L.1154), Santiago, Chile, Economic Commission for Latin America and the Caribbean (ECLAC).

Garay Salamanca, Luis Jorge (1998), "Colombia: estructura industrial e internacionalización, 1967-1996", *Programa de estudio sobre la industria de América Latina ante la globalización económica*, Luis Jorge Garay Salamanca (ed.), Santafé de Bogotá, Departamento Nacional de Planeación.

Hausman, Ricardo and others (1999), "Financial Turmoil and Choice of Exchange Rate Regime", OCE Working Paper, No. 400, Washington, D.C., Inter-American Development Bank (IDB).

Held, Günther (1994), "Liberalization or financial development?", *CEPAL Review*, No. 54 (LC/G.1845-P), Santiago, Chile.

_____(1993), "Bank regulation, liberalization and financial instability in Latin American and Caribbean countries", *Finance and the Real Economy: Issues and Case Studies in Developing Countries*, Yilmaz Akyüz and Günther Held (eds.), Santiago, Chile, Economic Commission for Latin America and the Caribbean (ECLAC) and World Institute for Development Economic Research (WIDER).

Hofman, André (1999a), "Economic growth and performance in Latin America", Reformas económicas series, No. 54 (LC/L.1350), Santiago, Chile, Economic Commission for Latin America and the Caribbean (ECLAC).

_____(1999b), "La inversión en América Latina: base de datos, 1950-1998", Santiago, Chile, Economic Commission for Latin America and the Caribbean (ECLAC), unpublished.

Hoshino, Taeko (1996), "Privatization in Mexico's public enterprises and the restructuring of the private sector", *The Developing Economies*, vol. 34, No. 1.

Katz, Jorge M. (2000), *Reformas estructurales, productividad y conducta tecnológica en América Latina*, Santiago, Chile, Economic Commission for Latin America and the Caribbean (ECLAC) and Fondo de Cultura Económica. (English translation: *Structural Reforms, Productivity and Technological Change in Latin America*, Santiago, Chile, ECLAC, 2001).

_____(1999a), "Cambios estructurales y evolución de la productividad laboral en la industria latinoamericana en el período 1970-1996", Reformas económicas series, No. 14 (LC/L.1171), Santiago, Chile, Economic Commission for Latin America and the Caribbean (ECLAC).

_____(1999b), "Reformas estructurales y comportamiento tecnológico: reflexiones en torno a las fuentes y naturaleza del cambio tecnológico en América Latina en los años noventa", Reformas económicas series, No. 13 (LC/L.1170), Santiago, Chile, Economic Commission for Latin America and the Caribbean (ECLAC).

Katz, Jorge (ed.) (1996) *Estabilización macroeconómica, reforma estructural y comportamiento industrial: Estructura y financiamiento del sector manufacturero latinoamericano en los años 90*, Buenos Aires, Alianza Editorial.

Kosacoff, Bernardo (1998), "Estrategias empresariales y ajuste industrial" (LC/BUE/R.230), Buenos Aires, Economic Commission for Latin America and the Caribbean (ECLAC).

Kosacoff, Bernardo and Fernando Porta (1997), "La inversión extranjera directa en la industria manufacturera argentina: tendencias y estrategias recientes", *Estudios de la economía real*, No. 3, Buenos Aires, Centro de Estudios para la Producción.

Latin American Weekly Report, London, weekly publication.

Lora, Eduardo (1997), "A decade of structural reforms in Latin America: What has been reformed and how to measure it", document presented to the Annual Meeting of the Board of Governos of the Inter-American Development Bank, Barcelona, Spain.

Lora, Eduardo and Felipe O. Barrera (1997), "A decade of structural reform in Latin America: Growth, productivity and investment are not what they used to be", OCE Working Paper, No. 350, Washington, D.C., Inter-American Development Bank (IDB).

Lüders, Rolf and Dominique Hachette (1992), *La privatización en Chile*, Santiago, Chile, International Center for Economic Growth (ICEG).

Mattar, Jorge and Wilson Peres (1999), "La inversión en México después de las reformas económicas", Santiago, Chile, Economic Commission for Latin America and the Caribbean (ECLAC), unpublished.

Mendiola, Gerardo (1999), "México: empresas maquiladoras de exportación en los noventa", Reformas económicas series, No. 49 (LC/L.1326), Santiago, Chile, Economic Commission for Latin America and the Caribbean (ECLAC).

Metal Statistics, Metallgesellschaft Aktiengesellschaft, Frankfurt, various issues.

Mizala, Alejandra (1992), "Las reformas económicas de los años setenta y la industria manufacturera chilena", *Colección estudios CIEPLAN*, No. 35, Santiago, Chile.

Moguillansky, Graciela (1999), *La inversión en Chile: ¿el fin de un ciclo de expansión?*, Santiago, Chile, Economic Commission for Latin America and the Caribbean (ECLAC)/Fondo de Cultura Económica.

_____(1998a), "Las reformas del sector de telecomunicaciones en Chile y el comportamiento de la inversión", Reformas económicas series, No. 4 (LC/L.1137), Santiago, Chile, Economic Commission for Latin America and the Caribbean (ECLAC).

_____(1998b), "Chile: las inversiones en el sector minero, 1980-2000", Reformas económicas series, No. 3 (LC/L.1131), Santiago, Chile, Economic Commission for Latin America and the Caribbean (ECLAC).

_____(1997a), "Chile: las reformas estructurales y la inversión privada en áreas de infraestructura", Reformas económicas series, No. 2 (LC/L.1083), Santiago, Chile, Economic Commission for Latin America and the Caribbean (ECLAC).

———(1997b), "La gestión privada y la inversión en el sector eléctrico chileno, Reformas económicas series, No. 1 (LC/L.1070), Santiago, Chile, Economic Commission for Latin America and the Caribbean (ECLAC).

———(1996), "The macroeconomic context and ivestment: Latin America since 1980", *CEPAL Review*, No. 58 (LC/G.1916-P), Santiago, Chile.

Montalbán, Krugger (1997), "Sigue el debate: ¿Nuevos impuestos a la minería?", Minería Chilena, No.198.

Montenegro, Diego and Alvaro Guzmán B. (1999), "Inversión y productividad en el sector agrícola agroindustrial boliviano: caso de la agricultura comercial en el período 1985-1998", Reformas económicas series, N° 43 (LC/L.1288), Santiago, Chile, Economic Commission for Latin America and the Caribbean (ECLAC).

Moreno-Brid, Juan Carlos (1999), "Reformas macroeconómicas e inversión manufacturera en México", Reformas económicas series, No. 47 (LC/L.1292), Santiago, Chile, Economic Commission for Latin America and the Caribbean (ECLAC).

Moussa, Nicole (1998), "Los cambios en la legislación sobre inversión extranjera directa en ocho países de América Latina", Santiago, Chile, Environment and Development Division, Economic Commission for Latin America and the Caribbean (ECLAC), unpublished.

Nelson, Richard R. (1991), "Why do firms differ, and how does it matter?", *Strategic Management Journal*, vol. 12, winter.

Nissanke, Machiko K. (1996), "Raising Finance for Enterprise: Theory and Evidence", paper prepared for the Expert Group Meeting for UNIDO's Global Report 1997.

Ocampo, José Antonio (1999), *La reforma del sistema financiero internacional: un debate en marcha*, Santiago, Chile, Economic Commission for Latin America and the Caribbean (ECLAC)/Fondo de Cultura Económica.

Oliveira, José Clemente de (1999), "Petróleo e gas natural: investimentos contidos, antes e durante as reformas", Brasilia, Economic Commission for Latin America and the Caribbean (ECLAC), unpublished.

Peres Núñez, Wilson (ed.) (1998), *Grandes empresas y grupos industriales latinoamericanos: expansión y desafíos en la era de la apertura y la globalización*, Mexico City, Siglo Veintiuno Editores.

Pindyck, Robert S. (1993), "Irreversibility, uncertainty, and investment", *Striving for Growth and Adjustment: The Role of Capital Formation*, Luis Servén and Andrés Solimano (eds.), Washington, D.C., World Bank.

———(1990), "Irreversibility and the explanation of investment behavior", *Stochastic Models and Option Values*, Amsterdam, North-Holland Publishing.

———(1988), "Irreversible investment, capacity choice, and the value of the firm", *American Economic Review*, vol. 78, No. 5.

Piñera Echeñique, José (1986), "Ley minera", *Estudios públicos*, No. 21, Santiago, Chile.

Rama, Martín (1993), "Empirical investment equations for developing countries", *Striving for Growth after Adjustment: The Role of Capital Formation*, Luis Servén and Andrés Solimano (eds.), Washington, D.C., World Bank.

Ramírez, Juan Mauricio and Liliana C. Núñez (1999), "Reformas estructurales, inversión y crecimiento: Colombia durante los años noventa", Reformas económicas series, No. 45 (LC/L.1290), Santiago, Chile, Economic Commission for Latin America and the Caribbean (ECLAC).

_____(1998), "Apertura y competitividad de la industria colombiana", *Coyuntura económica*, vol. 28, No. 2, Santafé de Bogotá, Colombia.

Romero, Carlos A. (1998), "Regulación e inversiones en el sector eléctrico argentino", Reformas económicas series, No. 5 (LC/L.1145), Santiago, Chile, Economic Commission for Latin America and the Caribbean (ECLAC).

Rodríguez, P. Víctor (1999), "Impacto de la reforma económica sobre las inversiones de la industria eléctrica en México: el regreso del capital privado como palanca de desarrollo", Reformas económicas series, No. 18 (LC/L.1175), Santiago, Chile, Economic Commission for Latin America and the Caribbean (ECLAC).

Sánchez Albavera, Fernando and others (1998), "Panorama minero de América Latina: la inversión en la década de los noventa", Medio ambiente y desarrollo series, No. 11 (LC/L.1148), Santiago, Chile, Economic Commission for Latin America and the Caribbean (ECLAC).

Scheinver, Isaac (1999), "Las carreteras y el sistema portuario frente a las reformas económicas en México", Reformas económicas series, No. 20 (LC/L.1196), Santiago, Chile, Economic Commission for Latin America and the Caribbean (ECLAC).

Schmidt-Hebbel, Klaus and others (1996), "Ahorro inversión y crecimiento en países en desarrollo: una panorámica" *Pensamiento iberoamericano*, No. 29, Madrid.

Servén, Luis and Andrés Solimano (eds.) (1993), *Striving for Growth after Adjustment: The Role of Capital Formation*, Washington, D.C., World Bank.

Silva, Francisca (1999), "La inversión en el sector agroindustrial chileno", Reformas económicas series, No. 46 (LC/L.1291), Santiago, Chile, Economic Commission for Latin America and the Caribbean (ECLAC).

Soares, Sebastião (1998), "Mineração: investimentos deprimidos, e indefinições quanto a recuperação pos-privatização", Brasilia, Economic Commission for Latin America and the Caribbean (ECLAC), unpublished.

Stallings, Barbara and Wilson Peres (2000), *Growth, Employment and Equity: The Impact of the Economic Reforms in Latin America and the Caribbean*, Washington, D.C., The Brookings Institution/Economic Commission for Latin America and the Caribbean (ECLAC).

Torres Flores, Ramón C. (1999), "México: impacto de las reformas estructurales en la formación de capital del sector petrolero", Reformas económicas series, No. 19 (LC/L.1196), Santiago, Chile, Economic Commission for Latin America and the Caribbean (ECLAC).

Wang, Lucía and others (1998), "Expectativas empresariales frente a las negociaciones del ALCA", *Ensayos sobre la inserción regional de la Argentina*, Working Paper, No. 81 (LC/BUE/L.164), Buenos Aires, Economic Commission for Latin America and the Caribbean (ECLAC).

ANNEX

ANNEX

Table A-1
TOTAL GROSS FIXED INVESTMENT, 1950-1998
(percentage of GDP in constant 1980 prices)

YEAR	ARGENTINA	BOLIVIA	BRAZIL	CHILE	COLOMBIA	COSTA RICA	MEXICO	PERU
1950	15.47	9.07	18.77	19.05	16.01	16.05	14.83	18.31
1951	18.31	12.24	21.65	20.76	15.41	15.51	17.49	19.82
1952	17.17	12.47	21.59	20.59	15.62	18.16	17.61	20.89
1953	16.11	7.75	17.67	19.76	19.92	18.10	16.10	23.07
1954	14.85	10.16	17.30	19.06	21.69	18.98	15.85	20.22
1955	16.10	15.85	15.46	22.09	22.07	17.77	16.57	21.98
1956	16.67	15.60	16.14	20.92	20.12	17.20	18.26	25.96
1957	17.37	14.81	16.92	21.67	14.76	15.27	18.40	27.07
1958	17.84	11.42	16.65	20.77	13.70	15.91	16.55	24.07
1959	15.10	11.86	17.87	17.99	13.72	15.88	16.08	18.87
1960	21.15	13.26	16.96	21.87	15.50	14.47	17.20	17.83
1961	23.03	10.85	16.13	21.14	16.01	14.95	16.52	20.69
1962	21.36	16.30	15.90	22.66	15.24	16.68	16.64	21.97
1963	18.59	15.93	15.24	24.46	13.58	16.33	17.18	19.94
1964	18.75	15.62	15.02	22.56	14.39	15.05	18.51	18.38
1965	17.99	16.09	14.24	21.03	13.12	16.98	18.66	20.56
1966	18.51	13.38	16.47	19.53	14.19	16.07	19.00	21.27
1967	18.98	14.33	16.00	19.32	14.82	16.59	20.33	18.83
1968	20.52	19.60	17.50	20.41	15.92	15.45	20.61	16.18
1969	22.74	15.83	19.27	20.67	16.42	16.12	20.81	16.32
1970	22.77	15.19	20.57	21.57	17.34	18.39	21.08	16.81
1971	23.79	15.92	21.31	19.33	17.16	19.96	19.89	18.20
1972	23.62	16.59	22.22	15.64	15.62	19.40	20.57	18.39
1973	21.18	15.34	23.58	14.99	15.91	19.53	21.78	23.78
1974	20.96	16.19	24.70	16.44	16.35	20.31	22.14	27.54
1975	21.19	18.11	25.77	14.89	15.37	19.65	22.91	27.58
1976	23.46	18.05	25.02	12.32	16.07	23.03	22.08	23.34
1977	26.74	18.30	23.56	13.59	15.54	23.78	19.91	21.36
1978	24.16	19.91	23.51	14.78	15.66	24.19	21.18	19.43
1979	24.17	18.49	22.88	15.84	15.43	26.58	23.33	20.18
1980	25.05	14.25	23.56	18.64	16.77	23.90	24.76	23.49
1981	22.57	13.77	21.62	20.70	17.43	18.36	26.46	26.10
1982	18.69	10.24	19.98	14.16	17.78	14.30	22.15	25.50
1983	18.01	9.14	17.22	12.25	17.71	15.05	16.58	20.46
1984	17.20	10.18	16.31	14.54	17.35	17.57	17.03	18.36

Table A-1 continued

Year	Argentina	Bolivia	Brazil	Chile	Colombia	Costa Rica	Mexico	Peru
1985	15.84	12.37	16.44	15.79	15.95	18.38	17.91	15.93
1986	16.48	13.37	18.76	15.31	16.22	19.51	16.41	17.28
1987	18.39	13.66	17.87	17.48	15.52	20.53	16.09	18.90
1988	17.47	13.60	17.00	18.60	16.53	19.13	16.81	17.80
1989	14.73	12.84	16.67	21.87	15.15	20.89	17.06	16.19
1990	12.66	13.94	15.53	21.62	14.04	23.10	18.37	17.46
1991	15.07	15.77	14.65	19.99	12.92	19.69	19.57	17.36
1992	18.24	17.39	13.81	22.08	13.96	22.25	20.93	18.17
1993	19.92	17.11	14.09	24.34	18.02	25.69	20.01	19.21
1994	22.35	15.04	15.41	24.45	20.71	22.59	20.77	22.30
1995	19.61	16.35	16.28	27.30	20.29	21.58	15.71	24.73
1996	20.48	17.50	16.36	27.87	18.26	20.33	17.38	23.14
1997	23.90	21.91	17.41	29.47	17.94	22.98	19.70	25.43
1998	24.45	26.46	16.94	28.90	15.44	26.77	20.80	25.23

Source: André Hofman, "La inversión en América Latina: base de datos, 1950-1998", Santiago, Chile, Economic Commission for Latin America and the Caribbean (ECLAC), unpublished.

Table A-2
GROSS FIXED INVESTMENT IN MACHINERY AND EQUIPMENT, 1950-1998
(percentage of GDP in constant 1980 prices)

YEAR	ARGENTINA	BOLIVIA	BRAZIL	CHILE	COLOMBIA	COSTA RICA	MEXICO	PERU
1950	2.56	4.3	9.18	6.22	6.34	4.10	2.67	7.32
1951	3.80	5.9	12.32	7.13	6.78	3.97	3.28	8.26
1952	3.49	6.0	11.23	7.01	6.85	4.64	3.08	8.50
1953	3.14	3.7	6.34	5.97	9.82	4.63	3.15	8.24
1954	2.86	4.9	7.57	5.25	10.08	4.86	2.91	6.53
1955	3.60	7.6	6.00	6.59	10.21	4.55	3.12	6.51
1956	3.93	7.5	6.22	7.65	8.85	4.38	3.35	9.47
1957	4.08	7.1	7.07	9.22	4.84	3.96	3.44	10.30
1958	3.94	6.0	6.64	9.00	4.54	3.99	3.01	8.56
1959	3.39	6.0	7.61	6.32	4.21	4.13	3.01	7.67
1960	5.96	6.6	6.65	7.46	6.15	3.87	3.08	7.30
1961	6.97	5.6	6.26	8.64	6.25	2.69	6.59	8.67
1962	6.52	9.5	6.21	7.82	5.63	3.75	6.64	9.88
1963	5.33	8.9	6.04	6.47	5.07	4.79	6.86	9.85
1964	5.51	8.7	5.87	6.91	5.75	5.27	7.39	8.41
1965	5.33	8.3	5.42	5.98	4.90	5.58	7.45	9.52
1966	5.40	6.5	6.93	6.66	5.54	6.08	7.58	10.06
1967	5.42	6.7	6.45	6.74	4.77	5.98	8.11	9.17
1968	5.72	10.8	7.18	7.44	5.43	4.96	8.22	7.98
1969	6.31	8.0	7.93	7.05	5.71	6.18	8.30	7.81
1970	6.26	7.7	8.55	7.29	6.86	8.20	8.41	7.70
1971	6.64	7.4	9.17	6.06	7.17	9.17	7.92	8.55
1972	6.92	8.0	9.43	4.71	6.58	8.97	8.24	8.01
1973	6.58	8.0	10.02	5.36	6.12	9.37	8.89	12.16
1974	6.21	8.8	11.02	4.99	6.39	9.51	9.28	14.74
1975	5.87	9.2	11.71	5.84	6.23	8.89	9.79	14.95
1976	6.20	9.0	10.96	4.97	6.83	10.26	9.04	11.39
1977	8.23	9.7	9.47	6.35	6.32	11.03	7.70	9.75
1978	6.53	10.2	9.25	7.19	6.86	11.75	8.39	8.32
1979	7.29	10.1	9.03	7.67	7.18	12.60	9.99	8.43
1980	8.06	8.2	8.96	8.62	7.72	10.19	10.87	10.87
1981	9.27	7.4	7.30	9.40	7.91	7.82	11.92	12.41
1982	6.83	6.7	6.12	5.90	7.99	5.58	8.47	11.62

Table A-2 continued

YEAR	ARGENTINA	BOLIVIA	BRAZIL	CHILE	COLOMBIA	COSTA RICA	MEXICO	PERU
1983	7.38	2.5	5.01	4.19	7.70	6.12	5.51	7.85
1984	7.76	4.4	4.86	4.55	7.29	7.54	5.93	6.30
1985	6.88	5.3	5.19	5.08	5.82	7.98	6.70	5.43
1986	7.29	5.7	6.42	4.64	6.09	9.05	5.92	5.48
1987	8.15	5.8	5.87	5.96	6.77	10.40	5.60	5.96
1988	7.56	5.7	5.36	6.70	7.06	9.24	6.57	4.47
1989	6.71	4.9	5.05	8.66	6.75	10.38	7.02	3.48
1990	5.96	6.1	4.55	8.03	6.65	12.72	8.01	3.82
1991	5.91	7.9	4.14	7.69	5.76	10.23	9.15	3.87
1992	7.15	8.7	3.90	8.89	6.41	12.67	10.24	3.88
1993	7.81	8.3	4.08	9.70	9.88	14.89	9.20	3.86
1994	8.76	6.5	5.12	10.20	10.81	12.11	9.66	4.51
1995	7.69	7.6	6.08	12.37	10.60	11.67	6.55	5.30
1996	8.03	8.6	6.11	12.44	9.53	11.00	7.66	5.12
1997	9.37	11.8	6.50	13.25	9.37	12.43	9.62	5.33
1998	9.59	15.2	6.32	12.99	8.06	15.31	10.73	4.99

Source: André Hofman, "La inversión en América Latina: base de datos, 1950-1998", Santiago, Chile, Economic Commission for Latin America and the Caribbean (ECLAC), unpublished.

Table A-3
GROSS FIXED INVESTMENT IN RESIDENTIAL AND
NON-RESIDENTIAL CONSTRUCTION, 1950-1998
(percentage of GDP in constant 1980 prices)

YEAR	ARGENTINA	BOLIVIA	BRAZIL	CHILE	COLOMBIA	COSTA RICA	MEXICO	PERU
1950	12.90	4.73	9.59	12.84	9.67	11.94	12.16	10.99
1951	14.51	6.38	9.33	13.63	8.63	11.54	14.21	11.57
1952	13.68	6.50	10.36	13.58	8.77	13.51	14.53	12.39
1953	12.97	4.04	11.33	13.79	10.10	13.47	12.95	14.84
1954	11.99	5.29	9.73	13.81	11.61	14.13	12.94	13.69
1955	12.50	8.26	9.46	15.50	11.86	13.22	13.45	15.46
1956	12.75	8.13	9.92	13.27	11.27	12.82	14.91	16.50
1957	13.30	7.72	9.85	12.46	9.92	11.30	14.96	16.78
1958	13.91	5.40	10.01	11.77	9.16	11.92	13.54	15.50
1959	11.72	5.89	10.26	11.67	9.52	11.76	13.07	11.20
1960	15.19	6.63	10.31	14.41	9.36	10.61	14.11	10.53
1961	16.05	5.26	9.86	12.50	9.75	12.27	9.93	12.02
1962	14.84	6.80	9.68	14.84	9.61	12.92	10.00	12.09
1963	13.26	6.99	9.20	17.99	8.51	11.55	10.33	10.09
1964	13.24	6.88	9.15	15.65	8.64	9.79	11.13	9.97
1965	12.66	7.81	8.82	15.04	8.21	11.39	11.22	11.04
1966	13.11	6.90	9.54	12.86	8.64	9.99	11.42	11.21
1967	13.56	7.60	9.55	12.58	10.06	10.61	12.22	9.66
1968	14.80	8.78	10.33	12.98	10.49	10.49	12.38	8.20
1969	16.44	7.80	11.33	13.63	10.72	9.95	12.51	8.52
1970	16.51	7.49	12.01	14.27	10.47	10.19	12.67	9.11
1971	17.15	8.56	12.14	13.27	9.98	10.79	11.96	9.65
1972	16.70	8.62	12.79	10.93	9.04	10.43	12.33	10.38
1973	14.61	7.33	13.56	9.63	9.79	10.17	12.89	11.63
1974	14.75	7.40	13.68	11.46	9.96	10.80	12.86	12.79
1975	15.31	8.95	14.06	9.04	9.14	10.76	13.12	12.63
1976	17.26	9.04	14.05	7.34	9.23	12.77	13.03	11.96
1977	18.51	8.61	14.09	7.24	9.21	12.74	12.21	11.61
1978	17.63	9.70	14.26	7.59	8.80	12.45	12.79	11.11
1979	16.88	8.39	13.85	8.17	8.25	13.98	13.34	11.74
1980	16.99	6.02	14.60	10.01	9.06	13.71	13.89	12.61
1981	13.30	6.36	14.32	11.30	9.52	10.54	14.53	13.69
1982	11.85	3.57	13.86	8.26	9.78	8.71	13.68	13.89
1983	10.64	6.61	12.22	8.06	10.01	8.93	11.07	12.61

Table A-3 continued

Year	Argentina	Bolivia	Brazil	Chile	Colombia	Costa Rica	Mexico	Peru
1984	9.44	5.83	11.45	9.99	10.06	10.03	11.10	12.06
1985	8.96	7.08	11.25	10.71	10.12	10.41	11.21	10.50
1986	9.19	7.65	12.34	10.67	10.13	10.47	10.49	11.80
1987	10.24	7.82	12.00	11.53	8.75	10.14	10.50	12.93
1988	9.91	7.79	11.64	11.90	9.47	9.89	10.24	13.33
1989	8.02	7.95	11.62	13.21	8.40	10.51	10.04	12.71
1990	6.70	7.84	10.98	13.58	7.39	10.38	10.35	13.64
1991	9.16	7.89	10.51	12.30	7.16	9.46	10.40	13.50
1992	11.09	8.67	9.91	13.19	7.55	9.58	10.66	14.29
1993	12.11	8.79	10.01	14.64	8.14	10.80	10.79	15.34
1994	13.59	8.53	10.29	14.25	9.89	10.48	11.09	17.79
1995	11.92	8.73	10.20	14.92	9.70	9.90	9.16	19.73
1996	12.45	8.92	10.25	15.43	8.72	9.33	9.71	18.46
1997	14.53	10.12	10.91	16.22	8.57	10.54	10.06	20.29
1998	14.86	11.25	10.61	15.91	7.38	11.46	10.03	20.13

Source: André Hofman, "La inversión en América Latina: base de datos, 1950-1998", Santiago, Chile, Economic Commission for Latin America and the Caribbean (ECLAC), unpublished.

Table A-4
GROSS FIXED INVESTMENT IN NON-RESIDENTIAL
CONSTRUCTION, 1950-1998
(percentage of GDP in constant 1980 prices)

Year	Argentina	Bolivia	Brazil	Chile	Colombia	Costa Rica	Mexico	Peru
1950	5.73	3.4	5.50	6.00	5.80	9.59	9.48	6.68
1951	7.54	4.6	5.06	7.26	5.18	9.25	11.63	7.04
1952	6.41	4.7	5.86	7.37	5.26	10.85	11.79	7.53
1953	6.60	2.9	6.53	6.85	6.06	10.83	10.11	9.02
1954	5.54	3.8	5.45	6.09	6.97	11.34	10.00	8.32
1955	5.97	5.9	5.26	6.64	7.11	10.62	10.46	9.40
1956	6.08	5.8	5.57	7.47	6.76	10.37	11.81	10.03
1957	6.34	5.5	5.56	8.41	5.95	8.86	11.80	10.20
1958	6.64	4.3	5.72	8.09	5.49	9.87	10.24	9.43
1959	5.59	4.7	5.90	6.59	5.71	9.19	9.61	6.81
1960	7.22	5.3	6.00	8.35	5.61	7.88	10.58	6.40
1961	7.61	4.1	5.75	7.59	6.83	9.62	6.05	7.31
1962	7.00	5.3	5.61	8.38	6.73	10.16	5.92	7.35
1963	6.24	5.4	5.21	10.74	5.95	8.04	6.16	6.14
1964	6.20	5.3	5.16	9.84	6.05	7.40	7.03	6.06
1965	5.90	6.1	4.88	8.93	5.75	8.91	6.98	6.72
1966	6.08	4.9	5.39	7.19	6.05	7.78	7.06	6.82
1967	6.26	5.5	5.39	7.40	7.04	8.05	7.70	5.87
1968	6.81	6.0	6.04	7.23	7.34	7.30	7.79	4.99
1969	7.52	5.4	6.84	7.34	7.50	7.67	7.75	5.18
1970	6.79	5.2	7.30	8.24	7.23	7.80	7.77	5.54
1971	7.88	6.2	7.40	6.87	7.01	7.76	6.16	5.65
1972	8.11	6.1	7.96	5.49	6.55	8.02	6.76	6.21
1973	6.84	5.0	8.62	5.03	6.72	7.44	7.62	6.07
1974	6.46	5.0	8.74	6.26	7.09	8.13	7.99	6.16
1975	4.81	6.2	9.02	4.55	6.72	7.30	7.69	5.79
1976	7.20	6.3	9.06	3.83	6.77	9.58	7.28	6.00
1977	10.08	5.9	9.09	3.97	6.57	9.52	6.86	6.01
1978	8.86	6.7	9.20	4.99	5.97	8.89	8.19	6.85
1979	7.94	5.6	8.92	4.86	5.84	10.23	8.74	6.16
1980	7.94	3.9	9.51	5.66	6.80	9.95	9.45	6.59
1981	4.91	4.3	9.19	7.43	7.17	8.11	10.13	6.41
1982	4.51	2.0	8.80	5.39	7.37	6.79	9.18	6.59
1983	4.13	5.2	7.49	5.62	7.17	6.86	6.65	6.36

Table A-4 continued

YEAR	ARGENTINA	BOLIVIA	BRAZIL	CHILE	COLOMBIA	COSTA RICA	MEXICO	PERU
1984	2.88	4.3	6.93	7.74	7.29	7.53	6.62	6.43
1985	2.51	5.2	6.81	7.79	7.34	7.97	6.49	5.54
1986	2.56	5.6	7.53	7.39	7.31	7.91	5.66	6.34
1987	2.83	5.8	7.32	8.03	5.85	7.24	5.55	6.63
1988	2.72	5.7	7.10	8.01	6.77	6.77	5.41	7.28
1989	2.19	6.0	7.09	8.95	5.79	7.31	5.14	7.50
1990	1.82	5.7	6.70	9.42	5.07	7.93	5.08	7.95
1991	2.47	5.4	6.41	7.98	4.48	7.15	4.78	7.83
1992	2.97	6.0	6.04	8.56	4.66	7.36	4.65	8.25
1993	3.23	6.1	6.10	9.53	4.40	8.33	5.05	8.93
1994	3.60	6.2	6.28	9.12	5.60	7.96	5.12	10.11
1995	3.14	6.2	6.22	9.20	5.49	7.53	4.64	11.21
1996	3.25	6.2	6.25	9.58	4.94	6.98	4.72	10.49
1997	3.77	7.0	6.65	10.04	4.85	7.89	4.40	11.53
1998	3.83	7.7	6.47	9.88	4.18	8.36	4.06	11.44

Source: André Hofman, "La inversión en América Latina: base de datos, 1950-1998", Santiago, Chile, Economic Commission for Latin America and the Caribbean (ECLAC), unpublished.

Table A-5
GROSS FIXED INVESTMENT IN RESIDENTIAL
CONSTRUCTION, 1950-1998
(percentage of GDP in constant 1980 prices)

Year	Argentina	Bolivia	Brazil	Chile	Colombia	Costa Rica	Mexico	Peru
1984	9.44	5.83	11.45	9.99	10.06	10.03	11.10	12.06
1950	7.17	1.3	4.09	6.84	3.87	2.35	2.69	4.31
1951	6.97	1.8	4.27	6.37	3.45	2.29	2.57	4.53
1952	7.27	1.8	4.51	6.21	3.51	2.66	2.73	4.85
1953	6.37	1.1	4.80	6.94	4.04	2.65	2.84	5.81
1954	6.45	1.5	4.27	7.72	4.64	2.78	2.94	5.36
1955	6.53	2.3	4.20	8.85	4.74	2.61	2.99	6.06
1956	6.67	2.3	4.35	5.79	4.51	2.45	3.10	6.46
1957	6.96	2.2	4.28	4.05	3.97	2.45	3.16	6.57
1958	7.27	1.1	4.29	3.67	3.66	2.05	3.30	6.08
1959	6.12	1.2	4.36	5.08	3.81	2.56	3.46	4.39
1960	7.97	1.3	4.30	6.06	3.74	2.73	3.53	4.13
1961	8.44	1.1	4.11	4.91	2.93	2.65	3.88	4.71
1962	7.84	1.5	4.07	6.45	2.88	2.76	4.08	4.74
1963	7.02	1.5	3.99	7.25	2.55	3.51	4.16	3.95
1964	7.04	1.6	4.00	5.80	2.59	2.39	4.10	3.90
1965	6.77	1.7	3.94	6.12	2.46	2.48	4.24	4.33
1966	7.03	2.0	4.16	5.67	2.59	2.21	4.36	4.39
1967	7.30	2.1	4.16	5.18	3.02	2.56	4.52	3.78
1968	7.99	2.8	4.29	5.75	3.15	3.19	4.60	3.21
1969	8.91	2.4	4.49	6.29	3.22	2.28	4.76	3.34
1970	9.71	2.3	4.72	6.03	3.24	2.38	4.90	3.57
1971	9.27	2.4	4.74	6.40	2.98	3.03	5.81	4.00
1972	8.59	2.5	4.83	5.43	2.49	2.41	5.58	4.17
1973	7.77	2.3	4.94	4.60	3.07	2.73	5.27	5.56
1974	8.29	2.4	4.94	5.20	2.87	2.67	4.87	6.64
1975	10.51	2.7	5.05	4.49	2.41	3.46	5.43	6.85
1976	10.06	2.7	4.99	3.51	2.46	3.19	5.75	5.96
1977	8.43	2.7	5.01	3.28	2.64	3.23	5.35	5.61
1978	8.76	3.0	5.06	2.60	2.83	3.55	4.60	4.27
1979	8.95	2.8	4.93	3.31	2.40	3.75	4.60	5.59
1980	9.04	2.1	5.09	4.35	2.26	3.75	4.44	6.02
1981	8.39	2.1	5.13	3.87	2.35	2.43	4.41	7.28
1982	7.34	1.5	5.06	2.87	2.41	1.92	4.50	7.30

Table A-5 continued

Year	Argentina	Bolivia	Brazil	Chile	Colombia	Costa Rica	Mexico	Peru
1983	6.51	1.4	4.73	2.44	2.84	2.07	4.42	6.25
1984	6.57	1.5	4.52	2.25	2.77	2.51	4.48	5.63
1985	6.45	1.9	4.44	2.92	2.78	2.44	4.72	4.96
1986	6.63	2.0	4.81	3.28	2.82	2.55	4.83	5.45
1987	7.41	2.0	4.68	3.50	2.90	2.89	4.95	6.31
1988	7.18	2.0	4.54	3.88	2.70	3.12	4.83	6.05
1989	5.83	2.0	4.53	4.26	2.61	3.19	4.90	5.21
1990	4.88	2.2	4.28	4.16	2.32	2.45	5.28	5.70
1991	6.69	2.5	4.10	4.32	2.68	2.31	5.62	5.67
1992	8.12	2.7	3.86	4.63	2.89	2.22	6.01	6.04
1993	8.88	2.7	3.90	5.11	3.74	2.47	5.75	6.42
1994	9.99	2.3	4.01	5.13	4.29	2.52	5.97	7.68
1995	8.79	2.5	3.98	5.73	4.21	2.37	4.51	8.52
1996	9.20	2.7	4.00	5.85	3.79	2.35	4.99	7.97
1997	10.75	3.1	4.25	6.18	3.72	2.66	5.66	8.76
1998	11.03	3.5	4.14	6.03	3.20	3.10	5.98	8.69

Source: André Hofman, "La inversión en América Latina: base de datos, 1950-1998", Santiago, Chile, Economic Commission for Latin America and the Caribbean (ECLAC), unpublished.

Table A-6
PUBLIC INVESTMENT, 1970-1998
(percentage of GDP in constant 1980 prices)

	Argentina	Bolivia	Brazil	Chile	Colombia	Costa Rica	Mexico	Peru
Year	1980	1980	1980	1980	1980	1966	1980	1979
1970	8.07	8.50	-	-	5.03	4.21	6.58	4.47
1971	8.55	9.40	-	-	5.44	5.08	4.85	4.20
1972	8.46	9.51	-	-	5.75	6.18	6.27	5.02
1973	6.80	6.13	-	-	5.46	5.59	8.07	5.89
1974	6.72	5.71	-	-	4.65	5.52	7.79	10.22
1975	7.74	7.42	-	-	5.19	6.25	8.97	8.53
1976	9.85	9.98	-	-	5.45	8.04	7.96	6.62
1977	9.93	11.44	9.49	-	9.02	9.68	8.24	4.72
1978	8.81	13.91	8.45	-	6.77	8.05	9.85	3.64
1979	7.46	11.50	6.93	-	6.71	8.59	10.60	5.28
1980	6.16	7.37	6.93	7.89	8.15	10.58	10.66	7.74
1981	5.50	6.49	7.24	7.47	8.72	8.67	12.00	8.73
1982	4.34	8.20	6.56	3.33	9.78	6.61	9.80	8.70
1983	5.20	6.38	5.20	3.98	10.14	7.90	6.55	6.59
1984	4.36	-	5.04	7.74	9.71	6.74	6.58	4.95
1985	4.03	-	5.29	6.98	9.01	9.83	6.47	4.13
1986	3.70	-	5.79	7.35	7.93	9.52	5.76	4.32
1987	5.70	6.10	5.30	7.18	7.61	8.39	4.96	5.08
1988	5.73	7.90	4.57	6.96	7.82	6.96	4.70	3.30
1989	4.39	8.50	3.71	5.83	7.36	7.72	4.71	4.20
1990	3.54	8.30	3.78	5.03	7.69	7.40	5.08	2.29
1991	2.20	8.70	4.95	5.48	7.48	6.30	4.69	3.79
1992	1.81	10.00	3.80	6.62	7.31	5.90	4.33	4.52
1993	2.13	9.20	4.40	5.83	9.56	6.00	4.15	5.46
1994	2.07	9.00	2.70	5.76	8.25	4.40	2.27	3.65
1995	1.14	8.50	2.50	4.80	8.72	4.88	1.84	3.60
1996	1.21	8.20	2.90	6.60	11.85	5.01	1.91	3.20
1997	1.18	7.20	-	6.20	12.30	5.66	1.95	3.20
1998	1.12	6.30	-	6.10	10.90	5.54	1.72	2.90

Source: Authors' compilation of figures from fiscal accounts of each country.
Note: Figures on public investment correspond in the case of Argentina and Mexico to Federal Government capital spending; in Bolivia, Chile, Colombia and Costa Rica to capital spending of the non-financial public sector; in Brazil to central public sector capital spending, and in Peru to central government capital spending. The calculations differ from national accounts methodology, so the figures should simply be used as a reference.

Table A-7
INVESTMENT IN DYNAMIC BRANCHES OF INDUSTRY

	LEVEL OF INVESTMENT			SHARE OF MANUFACTURING INVESTMENT		
	BRAZIL					
	PRE-REFORM	POST-REFORM		PRE-REFORM	POST-REFORM	
ISIC CLASSIFICATION	1970-1988	1992-1993	1995-1997	1970-1988	1992-1993	1995-1997
Food products	100.0	82.6	142.3	10.0	10.8	11.2
Other chemicals	100.0	23.7	218.3	1.2	0.4	1.8
Plastic products	100.0	56.6	196.4	2.3	1.8	3.6
Iron, steel and metal products	100.0	52.2	161.6	18.2	12.3	22.8
Electrical machinery	100.0	61.3	135.6	4.3	3.5	4.6
Transport equipment	100.0	43.0	227.2	7.7	4.3	13.4
Total	100.0	58.1	169.5	43.7	33.2	57.4
	CHILE					
	POST-REFORM			POST-REFORM		
ISIC CLASSIFICATION	1979-1985	1986-1989	1990-1995	1979-1985	1986-1989	1990-1995
Food products	100.0	172.0	365.5	35.7	41.3	28.8
Food products (312)	100.0	164.9	474.8	3.2	3.2	3.2
Drinks	100.0	170.4	481.0	5.8	7.7	6.5
Tobacco	100.0	74.2	175.7	2.1	1.2	0.9
Furniture	100.0	160.9	390.8	0.9	0.9	0.8
Paper and pulp	100.0	130.3	1094.8	14.0	10.9	27.2
Press and publications	100.0	99.3	243.1	6.8	4.5	3.6
Chemical industry	100.0	258.2	991.1	3.2	5.3	6.3
Plastic products	100.0	196.1	695.4	3.4	4.3	4.9
Glass	100.0	108.1	462.8	1.0	0.8	1.1
Other non-metal minerals	100.0	69.1	200.5	13.4	5.9	5.5
Iron and steel	100.0	104.2	402.1	4.3	3.4	3.6
Non-ferrous metals	100.0	299.4	797.2	0.8	1.8	1.6
Metal products	100.0	258.0	497.5	5.0	8.4	5.7
Scientific instruments	100.0	246.8	776.5	0.1	0.1	0.1
Other	100.0	91.1	259.3	0.4	0.2	0.2
Total	100.0	150.6	493.9	75.1	63.9	79.5

Table A-7 (continued)

ISIC CLASSIFICATION	LEVEL OF INVESTMENT				SHARE OF MANUFACTURING INVESTMENT		
	COLOMBIA						
	PRE-REFORM	POST-REFORM			PRE-REFORM	POST-REFORM	
	1970-1989	1990-1991	1992-1995		1970-1989	1990-1991	1992-1995
Food products	100.0	130.5	200.8		12.6	11.6	14.3
Food products (312)	100.0	134.3	290.6		2.4	2.4	4.2
Drinks	100.0	197.7	215.3		6.1	8.7	7.5
Clothing	100.0	115.2	197.0		1.8	1.4	1.9
Wood products	100.0	62.7	154.7		1.3	0.5	1.0
Paper and pulp	100.0	257.8	313.2		3.5	6.6	6.8
Other chemicals	100.0	153.9	271.3		3.7	4.0	5.5
Oil refineries	100.0	182.3	248.4		8.6	10.2	11.1
Oil and coal products	100.0	113.4	259.3		0.2	0.1	0.3
Rubber products	100.0	93.2	222.4		1.4	0.9	1.6
Plastic products	100.0	179.9	260.8		3.4	4.5	5.1
Glass	100.0	80.8	208.1		1.5	0.9	1.7
Other non-metal minerals	100.0	137.7	191.4		7.5	7.7	8.5
Metal products	100.0	76.8	130.5		3.8	2.0	2.7
Total	100.0	151.1	222.1		57.8	61.7	72.1

ISIC CLASSIFICATION	MEXICO						
	PRE-REFORM	POST-REFORM			PRE-REFORM	POST-REFORM	
	1970-1985	1986-1990	1991-1994		1970-1985	1986-1990	1991-1994
Food products	100.0	86.8	132.2		10.6	13.7	12.1
Drinks	100.0	72.1	155.3		4.9	5.1	6.4
Tobacco	100.0	81.3	265.3		0.4	0.5	1.0
Wood products	100.0	28.2	46.5		1.6	0.6	0.6
Other chemicals	100.0	104.0	174.0		6.6	9.7	9.7
Plastic products	100.0	59.1	110.4		2.9	2.5	2.8
Metal products	100.0	72.4	135.8		3.5	3.7	4.1
Electrical machinery	100.0	90.1	119.9		5.6	7.5	5.6
Transport equipment	100.0	94.1	236.0		9.5	13.9	19.0
Total	100.0	86.7	162.7		45.7	57.2	61.3

Table A-7 (continued)

ISIC CLASSIFICATION	LEVEL OF INVESTMENT			SHARE OF MANUFACTURING INVESTMENT		
	PERU					
	PRE-REFORM	POST-REFORM		PRE-REFORM	POST-REFORM	
	1972-1989	1992-1993	1994-1997	1972-1989	1992-1993	1994-1997
Food products	100	47.6	79.7	14.1	23.2	29.1
Textiles	100	41.0	19.2	18.7	25.7	9.7
Clothing	100	38.8	90.4	2.2	3.0	5.1
Leather Products	100	9.4	42.0	1.0	0.3	1.0
Wood products	100	n.a.	62.7	0.6	-0.1	0.9
Furniture	100	5.9	36.7	0.9	0.2	0.9
Paper and pulp	100	35.4	87.4	1.4	1.7	2.8
Chemical industry	100	26.5	25.9	5.7	5.1	3.5
Other chemicals	100	21.0	43.4	3.7	2.6	3.7
Other non-metal minerals	100	29.6	42.7	2.4	2.4	2.4
Metal products	100	17.5	50.8	4.5	2.5	5.3
Total	100	39.8	54.0	55.2	66.5	64.2

Source: Authors' compilation from the database of the research project.

Table A-8
PARTICIPATION OF FOREIGN OPERATORS IN PRIVATIZED
ELECTRICITY AND TELECOMMUNICATIONS SECTORS

SECTOR/INVESTMENT DESTINATION	TRANSNATIONAL OPERATORS	ORIGIN OF INVESTMENT
	ELECTRICITY SECTOR	
Argentina	Enersis	Chile/Spain
	Chilectra	Chile
	Endesa	Chile
	Gener	Chile
	Energy Corporation	United States
	Electricité de France	United States
Brazil	Enersis	Chile/Spain
	Endesa	Chile
	Chilectra	Chile
	Endesa España	Spain
	Gas Natural	Spain
	AES Corporation	United States
	Houston Industries Energy	United States
	Enron International	United States
	Southern Electric	United States
	Community Energy Alternatives	United States
	Electricité de France	France
	Iberdrola	Portugal
	Electricidad de Portugal	Portugal
	Pluspetrol	Argentina
	Tractebel	Belgium
Bolivia	Dominion Energy, Inc.	United States
	Energy Initiatives, inc.	United States
	Constellation Energy, inc.	United States
	Liberty Power Latin America	United States
	Cogentrix Anergy, inc.	United States
	Iberdrola	Portugal
Chile	Enersis	Chile/Spain
	Endesa	Chile
	Chilectra	Chile
	Gener	Chile
	Tractebel	Belgium
	Iberdrola	Portugal
	Power Market Developing Company	United States
Colombia	Gener	Chile
	Endesa	Chile
	Enersis	Chile/Spain
	Chilectra	Chile
	Endesa España	Spain

Table A-8 (continued)

SECTOR/INVESTMENT DESTINATION	TRANSNATIONAL OPERATORS	ORIGIN OF INVESTMENT
Peru	Dominion Energy	United States
	Energy Corporation	United States
	Gener	Chile
	Enersis	Chile
	Endesa	Chile
	Chilectra	Chile
	Chilquinta	Chile
	Endesa España	Spain
	Hidro Ontario	Canada
TELECOMMUNICATIONS SECTOR		
Argentina	Telefónica de España	Spain
	Equity Investment	United States
	Bellsouth	United States
	Motorola	United States
	Stet	Italy
	France Telecom	France
Brazil	ICI	
	Stet	Italy
	Telefónica de España	Spain
	Bellsouth, Motorola	United States
	Bell Canada, Telesystem	Canada
	Telia	Sweden
	Korea Mobile	Korea
Chile	Telefónica de España	Spain
	Stet	Italy
	Samsung	Japan
Colombia	Bell Canada	Canada
Mexico	Bell Atlantic	United States
	Loral Space Communications,	United States
	Hughes Communications	United States
Peru	Telefónica de España	Spain
	Bellsouth	United States

Source: Authors' compilation from the database of the research project.

Table A-9
INCOME FROM SALE OF PUBLIC UTILITIES FIRMS

	ELECTRICITY SECTOR			TELECOMMUNICATIONS SECTOR		
COUNTRY	FIRMS	MILLIONS OF DOLLARS	YEAR	FIRMS	MILLIONS OF DOLLARS	YEAR
Argentina	Segba	1 294	1 992	Telefónica	3 036	1990
	Hidronor	1 401	1992	Telecom	2 510	1990
	Transener	234	1992			
	Other provincial firms	676	1995			
Bolivia[a]	Corani	59	1995			
	Guaracachi	47	1995			
	Valle Hermoso	34	1995			
	Electropaz + Elfeo	65	1996			
	Elfec	50	1996			
	Ende	40	1997			
Brazil	Light Servicios de Electricidad	2 508	1996	Telefonía Móvil	7 542	.
	Cerj	588	1996	Área 1	2 450	1997
	Coelba	1 598	1997	Área 2	1 220	1997
	CDSA	714	1997	Área 3	1 330	1998
	Cia Centro Oeste de distribución de energía	1 372	1997	Área 4	457	1998
	Cia Norte, Nordeste de distribución de energía eléctrica	1 486	1997	Área 5	680	1998
	Cia Energética do Río Grande Do Norte	607	1997	Área 6	347	1998
	Coelce	868	1998	Área 7	314	1998
	Eletropaulo Metropolitana de Eletricidade S.A.	1 777	1998	Área 9	232	1998
				Área 10	512	1998

Table A-9 (continued)

Country	Electricity Sector			Telecommunications Sector		
	Firms	Millions of Dollars	Year	Firms	Millions of Dollars	Year
Chile [b]	Endesa	330	1986-1989	Telex Chile	n.a	1986
	Chilgener	0.05	1986-1987	CTC	212	1987-1989
	Chilectra	72	1983-1987	Entel	77	1986-1988
	Chilquinta	0.04				
	Colbun	n.a.	1996-1997			
	Edelaysen	Sale in progress				
	Edelnor	Sale in progress				
Colombia	Empresa de Energía de Bogotá (EEB)	1 230	1998			
	Central Hidroeléctrica Chivor	645	1997			
	Epsa	535	1997			
	Central Hidroeléctrica Betania	497	1997			
Mexico	Not privatized			Telmex	1 757	1990
				Iusacell	1 712	1997
				Satélites Mexicanos	692	1997
				Panamsat	650	1997
				Grupo MVS	120	1997
				Corporación Mobicom	54	1997
Peru [d]	Edegel	598.8	1995-1997	Entel Perú + Cptsa	2002	1994
	Cahua	48.5	1995-1997			
	Etevensa	203.4	1995-1997			
	Egenor	264.5	1995-1997			
	Empresa Eléctrica de Piura	19.7	1995-1997			
	Edelnor	209.3	1994-1997			
	Luz del Sur	406.9	1994-1997			
	Eléctrica de Chancay	10.5	1994-1997			

Table A-9 (continued)

| Country | Electricity sector | | | Telecommunications sector | | |
	Firms	Millions of Dollars	Year	Firms	Millions of Dollars	Year
Peru [d]	Eléctrica De Cañete	8.6	1994 - 1997			
	Electro Sur Medio	51.2	1994 - 1997			

Source: Authors' compilation from the database of the research project.

a/ Capitalization and management rights.

b/ Figures based on information collected by Luders and Hachette (1992) for 1986–1988. The last package of ENDESA shares was sold in 1989, so that income is not included in the figure.

c/ Peruvian sales generally correspond to 60% of the total shares in the firm, with the rest remaining in State hands. The figures do not include investment commitments.

Table A-10
PRICING LAWS AND THE EVOLUTION OF ELECTRICITY PRICES

Legislation	Pricing characteristics	Pricing history
Argentina		
Law 24 065 *Generation:* Open access for firms to Térmica Regulated hydroelectricity *Transmission:* Private monopoly, with open access to the network *Distribution:* Private monopoly, should satisfy all demand with obligatory access to third parties	*Generation:* Price determined in wholesale market, based on marginal cost of generating 1 MWH *Transmission:* Pay for energy transported, transport capacity and connection; toll payment, maximum income regulated, fixed annual amount recalculated every five years, plus complementary and connection charges. *Distribution:* Composed of two items: Cost of buying energy in wholesale market passed on to users Value added by distributor: fixing of maximum prices or price cap, based on average of wholesale and retail prices in the United States. Value added includes investment costs of expansion of repositioning of networks, operation and maintenance	Real annual reduction in the monomial price (energy plus power) of 6.2%, between 1992 and 1998, only in wholesale market
Bolivia		
Electricity law	*Generation:* Price is determined by short-term marginal cost of the companies plus a fixed price for investment in increasing capacity *Transmission:* Fixed maximum prices which include cost of operation, maintenance and administration plus an investment cost. *Distribution:* Price fixed based on rate of return to capital of 9% applied on net assets and working capital	Market began to set prices in May 1996 Sharp price volatility between May 1996 and December 1997 Market price (spot) of energy: decrease of 2.79% a year Price of power: increase of 38.07% a year

Table A-10 (continued)

LEGISLATION	PRICING CHARACTERISTICS	PRICING HISTORY
	Brazil	
Temporary regime 1995-2002	*Generation:* Transition rules, 1998-2003: Real 1998 prices held for four years 2002: Liberalization of 25% of price of energy sold a year Creation in 1998 of wholesale market *Transmission:* Maximum prices fixed in negotiations *Distribution:* Costs of generation and transmission markets, adjusted to maximum price regime or price cap and revised every 5 years	
	COLOMBIA	
Resolution Creg 218 of 1997: Changes price legislation for transmission Resolution Creg 031 of 1997: Fixed price for regulated consumers Decree 3087 of 1997: Creates solidarity and income redistribution fund and regulates solidarity contributions and subsidies on public services	*Unregulated consumers:* 0.5 MW of power or 270 MW/month of energy: Set by supply and demand *Prices for regulated consumers:* Prices after 1998 included economic costs generated throughout the production chain. These prices are adjusted through a maximum price (price cap) set until 2000. Residential consumers on low-incomes receive subsidies which reduce the price, while high-income residences, manufacturing and commerce pay surcharges.	

Table A-10 (continued)

Legislation	Pricing characteristics	Pricing history
Chile		
General electricity services law DFL 1 of 1982 Sets regulated prices Law 18922 de 1990 Transport system regulation	*Generation:* Free market rate: demand over 2 MW *Transmission:* Cost of toll covers annual operating and maintenance costs, plus investment assuming installations have useful life of 30 years, plus an annual income of 10% on investment considered to be new *Distribution:* Regulated prices for demand under 2 MW, depending on distribution system. Node prices: Biannual price review for power and energy in high voltage nodes. Weighted average of future marginal operating costs, needed to satisfy higher energy consumption. Prices should also finance an excess earned from investment in generation and transmission with a minimum annual rate of 10% Distribution rates: Determined every four years. Calculated on the basis of annual profitability of 10% on investment considered to be new, and on operating and maintenance costs of model distribution firms.	Distribution: Real annual drop of 9.2% between 1989 and 1995 Node price of the Metropolitan Region (hydroelectric generation): Real annual average drop of 5% between 1989 and 1995 Node price of the Second Region (hydroelectric generation): Real annual average drop of 12% between 1989 and 1995
Peru		
Electricity concessions law of 1992	*Generation:* Free market rate: Demand over 1 MW *Transmission:* Transport prices cover annual operation and maintenance costs, plus investments, assuming a useful of thirty years on all installations. For the cost of investment, an annual rent of 12% of the replacement value is applied. *Distribution:* High voltage price for demand below 1 MW: Biannual price review for power and energy in high voltage nodes. Weighted average of future marginal operating costs, needed to satisfy higher energy consumption. Prices should also finance an excess earned from investment in generation and transmission with a minimum annual rate of 12% *Distribution rates:* Calculated on the basis of annual profitability of 12% on investment considered to be new, and on operating and maintenance costs of model distribution firms.	Between 1993 and 1998 the high voltage price fell on average by 0.6% a year.

Table A-11

PRICING IN THE TELECOMMUNICATIONS SECTOR

LEGISLATION	CHARACTERISTICS OF PRICING
	ARGENTINA
Regulatory framework (1990) Reformulation of price setting mechanism (1992)	Absence of regulatory framework at the moment of privatization
	Negotiation with the private monopoly to maintain high rates during the period of compliance with the expansion and modernization programme
	Price cap system, with the price set in U.S. dollars and readjusted for inflation
	Allowance of cross-subsidies between national and international long distance services
	BOLIVIA
Telecommunications law (1995)	Price cap system, adjusted for inflationa and productivity
	The price cap is calculated as a weighted average of the prices of a basket of services. The productivity factor is recalculated every three years
	COLOMBIA
Regulated rates on local (resolution 087 de 1997), long distance (resolution 086 de 1997) and mobile telephone services	Long distance rates to be deregulated in 2001 Local service: Price cap system, which incorporates in the cost the hook-up charges, fixed charges and variable consumption charges. These costs are defined on the basis of the average reference cost, which is established by the regulatory body and adjusted for each operator, taking into account fixed and variable costs
	Cross-subsidies: The rate thus calculated does not incorporate subsidies and surcharges established for types of consumers.
	Long distance: Transition to a system of access charges based on costs

Table A-11 (continued)

LEGISLATION	CHARACTERISTICS OF PRICING
CHILE	
General telecommunications law (1982) DFL No 1,1987: Only non-competitive services are regulated	The price is set based on the incremental costs of providing service, including firms' plans for expansion over the next five years. If no expansion is planned, the price reflects the costs of exploitation and capital associated with the repositioning of company assets
MEXICO	
Rate regulation under consideration	Implementation of a new price and rate system planned for 1999 Currently, rates governed by the system inherited from the State monopoly in both basic and long distance service There is no accounting separation of the costs of service in the different markets, and cross-subsidies continue
PERU	
Regulation of basic and long distance services during the transition period	Negotiations with the private monopoly firm provide for a gradual rate adjustment, destined to eliminate cross-subsidies between the different types of phone service. Real rates regulated in the period 1994-1998

Source: Authors' compilation from the database of the research project.

ECLAC
publications

ECONOMIC COMMISSION FOR LATIN AMERICA AND THE CARIBBEAN
Casilla 179-D   Santiago, Chile

PERIODIC PUBLICATIONS

CEPAL Review

CEPAL Review first appeared in 1976 as part of the Publications Programme of the Economic Commission for Latin America and the Caribbean, its aim being to make a contribution to the study of the economic and social development problems of the region. The views expressed in signed articles, including those by Secretariat staff members, are those of the authors and therefore do not necessarily reflect the point of view of the Organization.

CEPAL Review is published in Spanish and English versions three times a year.

Annual subscription costs for 2001 are US$ 30 for the Spanish version and US$ 35 for the English version. The price of single issues is US$ 15 in both cases.

The cost of a two-year subscription (2001-2002) is US$ 50 for Spanish-language version and US$ 60 for English.

Revista de la CEPAL, número extraordinario: CEPAL CINCUENTA AÑOS, reflexiones sobre América Latina y el Caribe, 1998, 376 pp.

Síntesis estudio económico de América Latina y el Caribe, 1999-2000, 1999, 34 pp.

Summary Economic Survey of Latin America and the Caribbean, 1999-2000, 1999, 34 pp.

Balance Preliminar de las Economías de América Latina y el Caribe, 2000, 107 pp.

Preliminary Overview of the Economies of Latin America and the Caribbean, 2000, 107 pp.

Panorama Social de América Latina, 1999-2000, 312 pp.

Social Panorama of Latin America, 1999-2000, 312 pp.

La Inversión Extranjera en América Latina y el Caribe, 1999, 220 pp.

Foreign investment of Latin America and the Caribbean, 1999, 223 pp.

Panorama de la inserción internacional de América Latina y el Caribe, 1998, 246 pp.

Latin America and the Caribbean in the World Economy, 1998, 240 pp.

Estudio Económico de América Latina y el Caribe		*Economic Survey of Latin* *America and the Caribbean*	
1997-1998,	386 pp.	**1996-1997,**	335 pp.
1998-1999,	359 pp.	**1997-1998,**	360 pp.
1999-2000,	352 pp.	**1998-1999,**	326 pp.

(Issues for previous years also available)

Anuario Estadístico de América Latina y el Caribe /
Statistical Yearbook for Latin America and the Caribbean (bilingual)

1997,	894 pp.	*1998,*	880 pp.
1999,	851 pp.		

(Issues for previous years also available)

Libros de la C E P A L

1   *Manual de proyectos de desarrollo económico,* 1958, 5th. ed. 1980, 264 pp.
1   Manual on economic development projects, 1958, 2nd. ed. 1972, 242 pp. (Out of stock)
2   *América Latina en el umbral de los años ochenta,* 1979, 2nd. ed. 1980, 203 pp.
3   *Agua, desarrollo y medio ambiente en América Latina,* 1980, 443 pp.
4   *Los bancos transnacionales y el financiamiento externo de América Latina. La experiencia del Perú,* 1980, 265 pp.
4   Transnational banks and the external finance of Latin America: the experience of Peru, 1985, 342 pp.
5   *La dimensión ambiental en los estilos de desarrollo de América Latina,* Osvaldo Sunkel, 1981, 2nd. ed. 1984, 136 pp.
6   *La mujer y el desarrollo: guía para la planificación de programas y proyectos,* 1984, 115 pp.
6   Women and development: guidelines for programme and project planning, 1982, 3rd. ed. 1984, 123 pp.
7   *África y América Latina: perspectivas de la cooperación interregional,* 1983, 286 pp.
8   *Sobrevivencia campesina en ecosistemas de altura,* vols. I y II, 1983, 720 pp.
9   *La mujer en el sector popular urbano. América Latina y el Caribe,* 1984, 349 pp.
10   *Avances en la interpretación ambiental del desarrollo agrícola de América Latina,* 1985, 236 pp.
11   *El decenio de la mujer en el escenario latinoamericano,* 1986, 216 pp.
11   The decade for women in Latin America and the Caribbean: background and prospects, 1988, 215 pp.
12   *América Latina: sistema monetario internacional y financiamiento externo,* 1986, 416 pp. (Out of stock)
12   Latin America: international monetary system and external financing, 1986, 405 pp. (Out of stock)
13   *Raúl Prebisch: Un aporte al estudio de su pensamiento,* 1987, 146 pp.
14   *Cooperativismo latinoamericano: antecedentes y perspectivas,* 1989, 371 pp.
15   *CEPAL, 40 años (1948-1988),* 1988, 85 pp.
15   ECLAC 40 Years (1948-1988), 1989, 83 pp.
16   *América Latina en la economía mundial,* 1988, 321 pp. (Out of stock)

17 Gestión para el desarrollo de cuencas de alta montaña en la zona andina, 1988, 187 pp.

18 Políticas macroeconómicas y brecha externa: América Latina en los años ochenta, 1989, 201 pp.

19 CEPAL, Bibliografía 1948-1988, 1989, 648 pp.

20 Desarrollo agrícola y participación campesina, 1989, 404 pp.

21 Planificación y gestión del desarrollo en áreas de expansión de la frontera agropecuaria en América Latina, 1989, 113 pp.

22 Transformación ocupacional y crisis social en América Latina, 1989, 243 pp.

23 La crisis urbana en América Latina y el Caribe: reflexiones sobre alternativas de solución, 1990, 197 pp. (Out of stock)

24 The environmental dimension in development planning I, 1991, 302 pp.

25 Transformación productiva con equidad, 1990, 3rd. ed. 1991, 185 pp.

25 Changing production patterns with social equity, 1990, 3rd. ed. 1991, 177 pp.

26 América Latina y el Caribe: opciones para reducir el peso de la deuda, 1990, 118 pp.

26 Latin America and the Caribbean: options to reduce the debt burden, 1990, 110 pp.

27 Los grandes cambios y la crisis. Impacto sobre la mujer en América Latina y el Caribe, 1991, 271 pp.

27 Major changes and crisis. The impact on women in Latin America and the Caribbean, 1992, 279 pp.

28 A collection of documents on economic relations between the United States and Central America, 1906-1956, 1991, 398 pp.

29 Inventarios y cuentas del patrimonio natural en América Latina y el Caribe, 1991, 335 pp.

30 Evaluaciones del impacto ambiental en América Latina y el Caribe, 1991, 232 pp. (Out of stock)

31 El desarrollo sustentable: transformación productiva, equidad y medio ambiente, 1991, 146 pp.

31 Sustainable development: changing production patterns, social equity and the environment, 1991, 146 pp.

32 Equidad y transformación productiva: un enfoque integrado, 1993, 254 pp.

33 Educación y conocimiento: eje de la transformación productiva con equidad, 1992, 269 pp.

33 Education and knowledge: basic pillars of changing production patterns with social equity, 1993, 257 pp.

34 Ensayos sobre coordinación de políticas macroeconómicas, 1992, 249 pp.

35 Población, equidad y transformación productiva, 1993, 2nd. ed. 1995, 158 pp.

35 Population, social equity and changing production patterns, 1993, 153 pp.

36 Cambios en el perfil de las familias. La experiencia regional, 1993, 434 pp.

37 Familia y futuro: un programa regional en América Latina y el Caribe, 1994, 137 pp.

37 Family and future. A regional programme in Latin America and the Caribbean, 1995, 123 pp.

38 Imágenes sociales de la modernización y la transformación tecnológica, 1995, 198 pp.

39 El regionalismo abierto en América Latina y el Caribe, 1994, 109 pp.

39 Open regionalism in Latin America and the Caribbean, 1994, 103 pp. (Out of stock)

40 Políticas para mejorar la inserción en la economía mundial, 1995, 314 pp. (Out of stock)

40 Policies to improve linkages with the global economy, 1995, 308 pp.

41 Las relaciones económicas entre América Latina y la Unión Europea: el papel de los servicios exteriores, 1996, 300 pp.

42 Fortalecer el desarrollo. Interacciones entre macro y microeconomía, 1996, 116 pp.

42 Strengthening development. The interplay of macro- and microeconomics, 1996, 116 pp.

43 Quince años de desempeño económico. América Latina y el Caribe, 1980-1995, 1996, 120 pp.

43 The economic experience of the last fifteen years. Latin America and the Caribbean, 1980-1995, 1996, 120 pp.

44 *La brecha de la equidad. América Latina, el Caribe y la cumbre social,* 1997, 218 pp.

44 The equity gap. Latin America, the Caribbean and the social summit, 1997, 219 pp.

45 *La grieta de las drogas,* 1997, 218 pp.

46 *Agroindustria y pequeña agricultura: vínculos, potencialidades y oportunidades comerciales,* 1998, 180 pp.

47 *El pacto fiscal. Fortalezas, debilidades, desafíos,* 1998, 280 pp.

47 The Fiscal Covenant. Strenghts, weaknesses, challenges, 1998, 290 pp.

48 *Las dimensiones sociales de la integración regional en América Latina,* Rolando Franco y Armando Di Filippo, 1999, 238 pp.

49 *Teorías y metáforas sobre el desarrollo territorial,* Sergio Boisier, 1999, 128 pp.

50 *Privatización portuaria: bases, alternativas y consecuencias,* 1999, 248 pp.

51 *Nuevas políticas comerciales en América Latina y Asia. Algunos casos nacionales,* 1999, 584 pp.

52 *Un examen de la migración internacional en la Comunidad Andina,* 1999, 114 pp.

53 *Transformaciones recientes en el sector agropecuario brasileño,* M. Beatriz de A. David, Philippe Waniez, Violette Brustlein, Enali M. De Biaggi, Paula de Andrade Rollo and Monica dos Santos Rodrigues, 1999, 127 pp.

54 *La CEPAL en sus 50 años. Notas de un seminario conmemorativo,* 2000, 149 pp.

55 Financial globalization and the emerging economies, José Antonio Ocampo, Stefano Zamagni, Ricardo Ffrench-Davis y Carlo Pietrobelli, 2000, 328 pp.

57 *Las mujeres chilenas en los noventa. Hablan las cifras,* 2000, 214 pp.

MONOGRAPH SERIES

Cuadernos de la C E P A L

1 *América Latina: el nuevo escenario regional y mundial / Latin America: the new regional and world setting,* (bilingual), 1975, 2nd. ed. 1985, 103 pp.

2 *Las evoluciones regionales de la estrategia internacional del desarrollo,* 1975, 2nd. ed. 1984, 73 pp.

2 Regional appraisals of the international development strategy, 1975, 2nd. ed. 1985, 82 pp.

3 *Desarrollo humano, cambio social y crecimiento en América Latina,* 1975, 2nd. ed. 1984, 103 pp.

4 *Relaciones comerciales, crisis monetaria e integración económica en América Latina,* 1975, 85 pp.

5 *Síntesis de la segunda evaluación regional de la estrategia internacional del desarrollo,* 1975, 72 pp.

6 *Dinero de valor constante. Concepto, problemas y experiencias,* Jorge Rose, 1975, 2nd. ed. 1984, 43 pp.

7 *La coyuntura internacional y el sector externo,* 1975, 2nd. ed. 1983, 106 pp.

8 *La industrialización latinoamericana en los años setenta,* 1975, 2nd. ed. 1984, 116 pp.

9 *Dos estudios sobre inflación 1972-1974. La inflación en los países centrales. América Latina y la inflación importada,* 1975, 2nd. ed. 1984, 57 pp.

s/n Canada and the foreign firm, D. Pollock, 1976, 43 pp.

10 *Reactivación del mercado común centroamericano,* 1976, 2nd. ed. 1984, 149 pp.

11 *Integración y cooperación entre países en desarrollo en el ámbito agrícola,* Germánico Salgado, 1976, 2nd. ed. 1985, 62 pp.

12 *Temas del nuevo orden económico internacional,* 1976, 2nd. ed. 1984, 85 pp.

13 *En torno a las ideas de la CEPAL: desarrollo, industrialización y comercio exterior*, 1977, 2nd. ed. 1985, 57 pp.

14 *En torno a las ideas de la CEPAL: problemas de la industrialización en América Latina*, 1977, 2nd. ed. 1984, 46 pp.

15 *Los recursos hidráulicos de América Latina. Informe regional*, 1977, 2nd. ed. 1984, 75 pp.

15 The water resources of Latin America. Regional report, 1977, 2nd. ed. 1985, 79 pp.

16 *Desarrollo y cambio social en América Latina*, 1977, 2nd. ed. 1984, 59 pp.

17 *Estrategia internacional de desarrollo y establecimiento de un nuevo orden económico internacional*, 1977, 3rd. ed. 1984, 61 pp.

17 International development strategy and establishment of a new international economic order, 1977, 3rd. ed. 1985, 59 pp.

18 *Raíces históricas de las estructuras distributivas de América Latina*, A. di Filippo, 1977, 2nd. ed. 1983, 64 pp.

19 *Dos estudios sobre endeudamiento externo*, C. Massad and R. Zahler, 1977, 2nd. ed. 1986, 66 pp.

s/n United States – Latin American trade and financial relations: some policy recommendations, S. Weintraub, 1977, 44 pp.

20 *Tendencias y proyecciones a largo plazo del desarrollo económic o de América Latina*, 1978, 3rd. ed. 1985, 134 pp.

21 *25 años en la agricultura de América Latina: rasgos principales 1950-1975*, 1978, 2nd. ed. 1983, 124 pp.

22 *Notas sobre la familia como unidad socioeconómica*, Carlos A. Borsotti, 1978, 2nd. ed. 1984, 60 pp.

23 *La organización de la información para la evaluación del desarrollo*, Juan Sourrouille, 1978, 2nd. ed. 1984, 61 pp.

24 *Contabilidad nacional a precios constantes en América Latina*, 1978, 2nd. ed. 1983, 60 pp.

s/n Energy in Latin America: The Historical Record, J. Mullen, 1978, 66 pp.

25 *Ecuador: desafíos y logros de la política económica en la fase de expansión petrolera*, 1979, 2nd. ed. 1984, 153 pp.

26 *Las transformaciones rurales en América Latina: ¿desarrollo social o marginación?*, 1979, 2nd. ed. 1984, 160 pp.

27 *La dimensión de la pobreza en América Latina*, Oscar Altimir, 1979, 2nd. ed. 1983, 89 pp. (Out of stock)

28 *Organización institucional para el control y manejo de la deuda externa. El caso chileno*, Rodolfo Hoffman, 1979, 35 pp.

29 *La política monetaria y el ejuste de la balanza de pagos: tres estudios*, 1979, 2nd. ed. 1984, 61 pp.

29 Monetary policy and balance of payments adjustment: three studies, 1979, 60 pp. (Out of stock)

30 *América Latina: las evaluaciones regionales de la estrategia internacional del desarrollo en los años setenta*, 1979, 2nd. ed. 1982, 237 pp.

31 *Educación, imágenes y estilos de desarrollo*, G. Rama, 1979, 2nd. ed. 1982, 72 pp.

32 *Movimientos internacionales de capitales*, R. H. Arriazu, 1979, 2nd. ed. 1984, 90 pp.

33 *Informe sobre las inversiones directas extranjeras en América Latina*, A. E. Calcagno, 1980, 2nd. ed. 1982, 114 pp.

34 *Las fluctuaciones de la industria manufacturera argentina, 1950-1978*, D. Heymann, 1980, 2nd. ed. 1984, 234 pp.

35 *Perspectivas de reajuste industrial: la Comunidad Económica Europea y los países en desarrollo*, B. Evers, G. de Groot and W. Wagenmans, 1980, 2nd. ed. 1984, 69 pp.

36 *Un análisis sobre la posibilidad de evaluar la solvencia crediticia de los países en desarrollo*, A. Saieh, 1980, 2nd. ed. 1984, 82 pp.

37   Hacia los censos latinoamericanos de los años ochenta, 1981, 146 pp.

s/n **The economic relations of Latin America with Europe,** 1980, 2nd. ed. 1983, 156 pp.

38   Desarrollo regional argentino: la agricultura, J. Martin, 1981, 2nd. ed. 1984, 111 pp.

39   Estratificación y movilidad ocupacional en América Latina, C. Filgueira and C. Geneletti, 1981, 2nd. ed. 1985, 162 pp.

40   Programa de acción regional para América Latina en los años ochenta, 1981, 2nd. ed. 1984, 62 pp.

40   Regional programme of action for Latin America in the 1980s, 1981, 2nd. ed. 1984, 57 pp.

41   El desarrollo de América Latina y sus repercusiones en la educación. Alfabetismo y escolaridad básica, 1982, 246 pp.

42   América Latina y la economía mundial del café, 1982, 95 pp.

43   El ciclo ganadero y la economía argentina, 1983, 160 pp.

44   Las encuestas de hogares en América Latina, 1983, 122 pp.

45   Las cuentas nacionales en América Latina y el Caribe, 1983, 100 pp.

45   National accounts in Latin America and the Caribbean, 1983, 97 pp.

46   Demanda de equipos para generación, transmisión y transformación eléctrica en América Latina, 1983, 193 pp.

47   La economía de América Latina en 1982: evolución general, política cambiaria y renegociación de la deuda externa, 1984, 104 pp.

48   Políticas de ajuste y renegociación de la deuda externa en América Latina, 1984, 102 pp.

49   La economía de América Latina y el Caribe en 1983: evolución general, crisis y procesos de ajuste, 1985, 95 pp.

49   The economy of Latin America and the Caribbean in 1983: main trends, the impact of the crisis and the adjustment processes, 1985, 93 pp.

50   La CEPAL, encarnación de una esperanza de América Latina, Hernán Santa Cruz, 1985, 77 pp.

51   Hacia nuevas modalidades de cooperación económica entre América Latina y el Japón, 1986, 233 pp.

51   Towards new forms of economic co-operation between Latin America and Japan, 1987, 245 pp.

52   Los conceptos básicos del transporte marítimo y la situación de la actividad en América Latina, 1986, 112 pp.

52   Basic concepts of maritime transport and its present status in Latin America and the Caribbean, 1987, 114 pp.

53   Encuestas de ingresos y gastos. Conceptos y métodos en la experiencia latinoamericana. 1986, 128 pp.

54   Crisis económica y políticas de ajuste, estabilización y crecimiento, 1986, 123 pp.

54   The economic crisis: Policies for adjustment, stabilization and growth, 1986, 125 pp.

55   El desarrollo de América Latina y el Caribe: escollos, requisitos y opciones, 1987, 184 pp.

55   Latin American and Caribbean development: obstacles, requirements and options, 1987, 184 pp.

56   Los bancos transnacionales y el endeudamiento externo en la Argentina, 1987, 112 pp.

57   El proceso de desarrollo de la pequeña y mediana empresa y su papel en el sistema industrial: el caso de Italia, 1988, 112 pp.

58   La evolución de la economía de América Latina en 1986, 1987, 99 pp.

58   The evolution of the Latin American Economy in 1986, 1988, 95 pp.

59   Protectionism: regional negotiation and defence strategies, 1988, 261 pp.

60   Industrialización en América Latina: de la "caja negra" al "casillero vacío", F. Fajnzylber, 1989, 2nd. ed. 1990, 176 pp.

60 *Industrialization in Latin America: from the "Black Box" to the "Empty Box"*, F. Fajnzylber, 1990, 172 pp.

61 *Hacia un desarrollo sostenido en América Latina y el Caribe: restricciones y requisitos*, 1989, 94 pp.

61 *Towards sustained development in Latin America and the Caribbean: restrictions and requisites,* 1989, 93 pp.

62 *La evolución de la economía de América Latina en 1987,* 1989, 87 pp.

62 *The evolution of the Latin American economy in 1987,* 1989, 84 pp.

63 *Elementos para el diseño de políticas industriales y tecnológicas en América Latina,* 1990, 2nd. ed. 1991, 172 pp.

64 *La industria de transporte regular internacional y la competitividad del comercio exterior de los países de América Latina y el Caribe,* 1989, 132 pp.

64 *The international common-carrier transportation industry and the competitiveness of the foreign trade of the countries of Latin America and the Caribbean,* 1989, 116 pp.

65 *Cambios estructurales en los puertos y la competitividad del comercio exterior de América Latina y el Caribe,* 1991, 141 pp.

65 *Structural Changes in Ports and the Competitiveness of Latin American and Caribbean Foreign Trade,* 1990, 126 pp.

66 *The Caribbean: one and divisible,* 1993, 207 pp.

67 *La transferencia de recursos externos de América Latina en la posguerra,* 1991, 92 pp.

67 *Postwar transfer of resources abroad by Latin America,* 1992, 90 pp.

68 *La reestructuración de empresas públicas: el caso de los puertos de América Latina y el Caribe,* 1992, 148 pp.

68 *The restructuring of public-sector enterprises: the case of Latin American and Caribbean ports,* 1992, 129 pp.

69 *Las finanzas públicas de América Latina en la década de 1980,* 1993, 100 pp.

69 *Public Finances in Latin America in the 1980s,* 1993, 96 pp.

70 *Canales, cadenas, corredores y competitividad: un enfoque sistémico y su aplicación a seis productos latinoamericanos de exportación,* 1993, 183 pp.

71 *Focalización y pobreza,* 1995, 249 pp. (Out of stock)

72 *Productividad de los pobres rurales y urbanos,* 1995, 318 pp. (Out of stock)

73 *El gasto social en América Latina: un examen cuantitativo y cualitativo,* 1995, 167 pp. (Out of stock)

74 *América Latina y el Caribe: dinámica de la población y desarrollo,* 1995, 151 pp.

75 *Crecimiento de la población y desarrollo,* 1995, 95 pp.

76 *Dinámica de la población y desarrollo económico,* 1997, 116 pp.

77 *La reforma laboral y la participación privada en los puertos del sector público,* 1996, 168 pp.

77 *Labour reform and private participation in public-sector ports,* 1996, 160 pp.

78 *Centroamérica y el TLC: efectos inmediatos e implicaciones futuras,* 1996, 164 pp.

79 *Ciudadanía y derechos humanos desde la perspectiva de las políticas públicas,* 1997, 124 pp.

80 *Evolución del gasto público social en América Latina: 1980-1995,* 1998, 200 pp.

81 *La apertura económica y el desarrollo agrícola en América Latina y el Caribe,* 1997, 136 pp.

82 *A dinámica do Setor Saúde no Brasil,* 1997, 220 pp.

83 *Temas y desafíos de las políticas de población en los años noventa en América Latina y el Caribe,* 1998, 268 pp.

84 *El régimen de contratación petrolera de América Latina en la década de los noventa,* 1998, 134 pp.

85 *Centroamérica, México y República Dominicana: maquila y transformación productiva,* 1999, 190 pp.

Cuadernos Estadísticos de la C E P A L

1 *América Latina: relación de precios del intercambio*, 1976, 2nd. ed., 1984, 66 pp.
2 *Indicadores del desarrollo económico y social en América Latina*, 1976, 2nd. ed. 1984, 179 pp.
3 *Series históricas del crecimiento de América Latina*, 1978, 2nd. ed. 1984, 206 pp.
4 *Estadísticas sobre la estructura del gasto de consumo de los hogares según finalidad del gasto, por grupos de ingreso*, 1978, 110 pp. (Out of print; replaced by No. 8 below)
5 *El balance de pagos de América Latina, 1950-1977*, 1979, 2nd. ed. 1984, 164 pp.
6 *Distribución regional del producto interno bruto sectorial en los países de América Latina*, 1981, 2nd. ed. 1985, 68 pp.
7 *Tablas de insumo-producto en América Latina*, 1983, 383 pp.
8 *Estructura del gasto de consumo de los hogares según finalidad del gasto, por grupos de ingreso*, 1984, 146 pp.
9 *Origen y destino del comercio exterior de los países de la Asociación Latinoamericana de Integración y del Mercado Común Centroamericano*, 1985, 546 pp.
10 *América Latina: balance de pagos, 1950-1984*, 1986, 357 pp.
11 *El comercio exterior de bienes de capital en América Latina*, 1986, 288 pp.
12 *América Latina: índices de comercio exterior, 1970-1984*, 1987, 355 pp.
13 *América Latina: comercio exterior según la clasificación industrial internacional uniforme de todas las actividades económicas*, 1987, Vol. I, 675 pp; Vol. II, 675 pp.
14 *La distribución del ingreso en Colombia. Antecedentes estadísticos y características socioeconómicas de los receptores*, 1988, 156 pp.
15 *América Latina y el Caribe: series regionales de cuentas nacionales a precios constantes de 1980*, 1991, 245 pp.
16 *Origen y destino del comercio exterior de los países de la Asociación Latinoamericana de Integración*, 1991, 190 pp.
17 *Comercio intrazonal de los países de la Asociación de Integración, según capítulos de la clasificación uniforme para el comercio internacional, revisión 2*, 1992, 299 pp.
18 *Clasificaciones estadísticas internacionales incorporadas en el Banco de Datos del Comercio Exterior de América Latina y el Caribe de la CEPAL*, 1993, 313 pp.
19 *América Latina: comercio exterior según la clasificación industrial internacional uniforme de todas las actividades económicas (CIIU) - Volumen I -Exportaciones*, 1993, 285 pp.
19 *América Latina: comercio exterior según la clasificación industrial internacional uniforme de todas las actividades económicas (CIIU) - Volumen II -Importaciones*, 1993, 291 pp.
20 *Dirección del comercio exterior de América Latina y el Caribe según principales productos y grupos de productos, 1970-1992*, 1994, 483 pp.
21 *Estructura del gasto de consumo de los hogares en América Latina*, 1995, 274 pp.
22 *América Latina y el Caribe: dirección del comercio exterior de los principales productos alimenticios y agrícolas según países de destino y procedencia, 1979-1993*, 1995, 224 pp.
23 *América Latina y el Caribe: series regionales y oficiales de cuentas nacionales, 1950-1994*, 1996, 130 pp.
24 *Chile: comercio exterior según grupos de la Clasificación Uniforme para el Comercio Internacional, Rev. 3, y países de destino y procedencia, 1990-1995*, 1996, 480 pp.
25 *Clasificaciones estadísticas internacionales incorporadas en el Banco de Datos del Comercio Exterior de América Latina y el Caribe de la CEPAL*, 1998, 287 pp.
26 *América Latina y el Caribe: series estadísticas sobre comercio de servicios 1980-1997*, 1998, 124 pp.

Estudios e Informes de la C E P A L

1 *Nicaragua: el impacto de la mutación política,* 1981, 2nd. ed. 1982, 126 pp.
2 *Perú 1968-1977: la política económica en un proceso de cambio global,* 1981, 2nd. ed. 1982, 166 pp.
3 *La industrialización de América Latina y la cooperación internacional,* 1981, 170 pp. (Out of print; will not be reprinted.)
4 *Estilos de desarrollo, modernización y medio ambiente en la agricultura latinoamericana,* 1981, 4th. ed. 1984, 130 pp.
5 *El desarrollo de América Latina en los años ochenta,* 1981, 2nd. ed. 1982, 153 pp.
5 **Latin American development in the 1980s,** 1981, 2nd. ed. 1982, 134 pp.
6 *Proyecciones del desarrollo latinoamericano en los años ochenta,* 1981, 3rd. ed. 1985, 96 pp.
6 **Latin American development projections for the 1980s,** 1982, 2nd. ed. 1983, 89 pp.
7 *Las relaciones económicas externas de América Latina en los años ochenta,* 1981, 2nd. ed. 1982, 180 pp. (Out of stock)
8 *Integración y cooperación regionales en los años ochenta,* 1982, 2nd. ed. 1982, 174 pp.
9 *Estrategias de desarrollo sectorial para los años ochenta: industria y agricultura,* 1981, 2nd. ed. 1985, 100 pp.
10 *Dinámica del subempleo en América Latina. PREALC,* 1981, 2nd. ed. 1985, 101 pp.
11 *Estilos de desarrollo de la industria manufacturera y medio ambiente en América Latina,* 1982, 2nd. ed. 1984, 178 pp.
12 *Relaciones económicas de América Latina con los países miembros del "Consejo de Asistencia Mutua Económica",* 1982, 154 pp.
13 *Campesinado y desarrollo agrícola en Bolivia,* 1982, 175 pp.
14 *El sector externo: indicadores y análisis de sus fluctuaciones. El caso argentino,* 1982, 2nd. ed. 1985, 216 pp.
15 *Ingeniería y consultoría en Brasil y el Grupo Andino,* 1982, 320 pp.
16 *Cinco estudios sobre la situación de la mujer en América Latina,* 1982, 2nd. ed. 1985, 178 pp.
16 **Five studies on the situation of women in Latin America,** 1983, 2nd. ed. 1984, 188 pp.
17 *Cuentas nacionales y producto material en América Latina,* 1982, 129 pp.
18 *El financiamiento de las exportaciones en América Latina,* 1983, 212 pp.
19 *Medición del empleo y de los ingresos rurales,* 1982, 2nd. ed. 1983, 173 pp.
19 **Measurement of employment and income in rural areas,** 1983, 184 pp.
20 *Efectos macroeconómicos de cambios en las barreras al comercio y al movimiento de capitales: un modelo de simulación,* 1982, 68 pp. (Out of stock)
21 *La empresa pública en la economía: la experiencia argentina,* 1982, 2nd. ed. 1985, 134 pp.
22 *Las empresas transnacionales en la economía de Chile, 1974-1980,* 1983, 178 pp.
23 *La gestión y la informática en las empresas ferroviarias de América Latina y España,* 1983, 195 pp.
24 *Establecimiento de empresas de reparación y mantenimiento de contenedores en América Latina y el Caribe,* 1983, 314 pp.
24 **Establishing container repair and maintenance enterprises in Latin America and the Caribbean,** 1983, 236 pp.
25 *Agua potable y saneamiento ambiental en América Latina, 1981-1990 / **Drinking water supply and sanitation in Latin America, 1981-1990*** (bilingual), 1983, 14 pp.
26 *Los bancos transnacionales, el estado y el endeudamiento externo en Bolivia,* 1983, 282 pp.
27 *Política económica y procesos de desarrollo. La e xperiencia argentina entre 1976 y 1981,* 1983, 157 pp.
28 *Estilos de desarrollo, energía y medio ambiente: un estudio de caso exploratorio,* 1983, 129 pp.
29 *Empresas transnacionales en la industria de alimentos. El caso argentino: cereales y carne,* 1983, 93 pp.

Serie INFOPLAN: Temas Especiales del Desarrollo

1 *Resúmenes de documentos sobre deuda externa*, 1986, 324 pp.
2 *Resúmenes de documentos sobre cooperación entre países en desarrollo*, 1986, 189 pp.
3 *Resúmenes de documentos sobre recursos hídricos*, 1987, 290 pp.
4 *Resúmenes de documentos sobre planificación y medio ambiente*, 1987, 111 pp.
5 *Resúmenes de documentos sobre integración económica en América Latina y el Caribe*, 1987, 273 pp.
6 *Resúmenes de documentos sobre cooperación entre países en desarrollo, II parte*, 1988, 146 pp.
7 *Documentos sobre privatización con énfasis en América Latina*, 1991, 82 pp.
8 *Reseñas de documentos sobre desarrollo ambientalmente sustentable*, 1992, 217 pp. (Out of stock)
9 *MERCOSUR: resúmenes de documentos*, 1993, 119 pp.
10 *Políticas sociales: resúmenes de documentos*, 1995, 95 pp.
11 *Modernización del Estado: resúmenes de documentos*, 1995, 73 pp.
12 *Gestión de la información: reseñas de documentos*, 1996, 152 pp.
13 *Políticas sociales: resúmenes de documentos II*, 1997, 80 pp.

Recent co-publications

On occasion ECLAC concludes agreements for the co-publication of texts that may be of special interest to other international organizations or to publishing houses. In the latter case, the publishing houses have exclusive sales and distribution rights.

Las nuevas corrientes financieras hacia América Latina: Fuentes, efectos y políticas, Ricardo Ffrench-Davis y Stephany Griffith-Jones (comp.), México, CEPAL/Fondo de Cultura Económica, primera edición, 1995.

Hacia un nuevo modelo de organización mundial. El sector manufacturero argentino en los años noventa, Jorge Katz, Roberto Bisang, Gustavo Burachick editores, CEPAL/IDRC/ Alianza Editorial, Buenos Aires, 1996.

América Latina y el Caribe quince años después. De la década perdida a la transformación económica 1980-1995, CEPAL/Fondo de Cultura Económica, Santiago, 1996.

Tendências econômicas e sociais na América Latina e no Caribe / Economic and social trends in Latin America and the Caribbean / *Tendencias económicas y sociales en América Latina y el Caribe*, CEPAL/IBGE/CARECON RIO, Brasil, 1996.

Flujos de Capital e Inversión Productiva. Lecciones para América Latina, Ricardo Ffrench-Davis -Helmut Reisen (compiladores). CEPAL/M. Graw Hill, Santiago, 1997.

Políticas para mejorar la inserción en la economía mundial. América y El Caribe, CEPAL/Fondo de Cultura Económica, Santiago, 1997.

La Economía Cubana. Reformas estructurales y desempeño en los noventa, Comisión Económica para América Latina y el Caribe. CEPAL/Fondo de Cultura Económica, México, 1997.

La Igualdad de los Modernos: reflexiones acerca de la realización de los derechos económicos, sociales y culturales en América Latina, CEPAL/IIDH, Costa Rica, 1997.

Estrategias empresariales en tiempos de cambio, Bernardo Kosacoff (editor), CEPAL/Universidad Nacional de Quilmes, Argentina, 1998.

Grandes empresas y grupos industriales latinoamericanos, Wilson Peres (coord.), CEPAL/Siglo XXI, Buenos Aires, 1998.

Cincuenta años de pensamiento en la CEPAL: textos seleccionados, dos volúmenes, CEPAL/Fondo de Cultura Económica, Santiago, 1998.

América Latina y el Caribe. Políticas para mejorar la inserción en la economía mundial, CEPAL/Fondo de Cultura Económica, Santiago, 1998.

Macroeconomía, comercio y finanzas para reformar las reformas en América Latina, Ricardo Ffrench Davis, CEPAL/Mc Graw-Hill, Santiago, 1999.

La reforma del sistema financiero internacional: un debate en marcha, José Antonio Ocampo, CEPAL/Fondo de Cultura Económica, Santiago, 1999.

La inversión en Chile ¿El fin de un ciclo de expansión?, Graciela Mouguillansky, CEPAL/Fondo de Cultura Económica, Santiago, 1999.

El gran eslabón: educación y desarrollo en el umbral del siglo XXI, Martín Hopenhayn y Ernesto Ottone, CEPAL/Fondo de Cultura Económica, Argentina, 1999.

La modernidad problemática: cuatro ensayos sobre el desarrollo Latinoamericano, Ernesto Ottone, CEPAL/JUS, México, 2000.

Brasil uma década em transição, Renato Baumann, CEPAL/ CAMPUS, Brasil, 2000.

Ensayo sobre el financiamiento de la seguridad social en salud, Tomos I y II, Daniel Titelman y Andras Uthoff, CEPAL/Fondo de Cultura Económica, Chile, 2000.

Integración regional, desarrollo y equidad, Armando Di Filippo y Rolando Franco, CEPAL/Siglo XXI, México, 2000.

Cinqüenta anos de pensamento na CEPAL, Tomos I y II, Ricardo Bielschowsky, CEPAL/RECORD/ COFECOM, Brasil, 2000.

Growth, employment, and equity. The impact of the Economic Reforms in Latin America and the Caribbean, Barbara Stallings and Wilson Peres, CEPAL/Brookings Institution Press, Washington, D.C., 2000.

Crecimiento, empleo y equidad. El impacto de las reformas económicas en América Latina y el Caribe, Barbara Stallings y Wilson Peres, CEPAL/Fondo de Cultura Económica, Santiago, 2000.

Reformas económicas, crecimiento y empleo. Los mercados de trabajo en América Latina y el Caribe, Jürgen Weller, CEPAL/Fondo de Cultura Económica, Santiago, 2000.

Reformas estructurales, productividad y conducta tecnológica en América Latina, Jorge Katz, CEPAL/Fondo de Cultura Económica, Santiago, 2000.

Inversión y reformas económicas en América Latina, Graciela Moguillansky y Ricardo Bielschowsky, CEPAL/Fondo de Cultura Económica, Santiago, 2000.

La distribución del ingreso en América Latina y el Caribe, Samuel Morley, CEPAL/Fondo de Cultura Económica, Santiago, 2000.